Lancashire

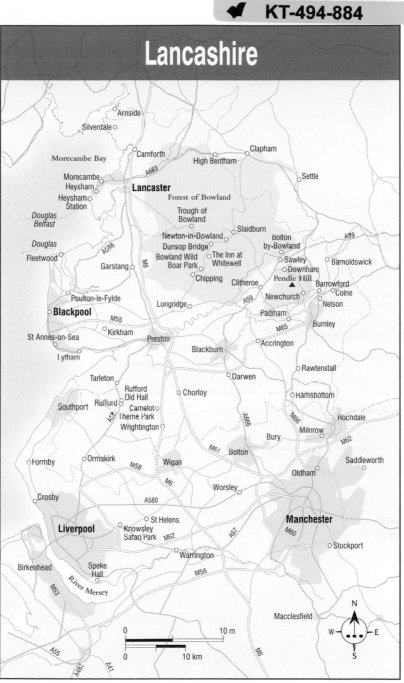

Contents

Lancashire has suffered almost as many boundary changes as Poland. In the reorganisation of local government in 1974, Widnes and Warrington were lost to Cheshire; Southport, Crosby and Liverpool became part of the new metropolitan county of Merseyside and almost all the former mill towns were swallowed up by the new metropolitan county of Greater Manchester.

The Forest of Bowland
One of Lancashire's best kept secrets

Top left to bottom right: Hark to Bounty, Slaidburn; Church at Chipping; Bridge near Whitewell; Easter Egg Festival, Newton in Bowland; The Inn at Whitewell

See pages 74–78

Left: Pendle Hill
Below: Fishing Boats on the River Lune
Bottom: Albert Dock and the Three Graces

While Lancashire's treasured Lakeland area, which had always featured so prominently in the county's calendars, was lost to Cumbria, there was some compensation in the acquisition from Yorkshire of Pennine lands on the western side of England's backbone.

For the purposes of this book, we'll grudgingly grant Widnes and Warrington to Cheshire and we'll even give the Lancashire Lakeland to Cumbria, as it seems to belong there, but we'll keep the rest, because it constitutes the land that most people still understand as Lancashire and is, in large measure, the area that was first designated as Lancashire in 1182. It is a county that stretches from the city of Manchester in the south to the top of Morecambe Bay in the north, and from Liverpool in the west to the Pennine watershed in the east.

We begin our visitor guide in Manchester, the world's first industrial city, which became the cotton capital of the globe and the heart of an industry that accounted for more than a quarter of Britain's entire export trade. Today it is equally famous, but for very different reasons. Known throughout the sporting world as the home of two of the richest clubs in football, it is also a thriving business centre and one of the world's most vibrant and exciting cities, with a wide range of visitor attractions for people of all ages, a plethora of fabulous buildings, both new and old, and a skyline that changes almost daily.

After sampling the many and varied delights of the city, we move into Greater Manchester and travel in an arc around the former mill towns, which collectively produced up to eight billion yards of cloth per year before the cotton industry went into decline. Once known as the 'workshop of the world', this area is still regarded by the uninformed as an unhealthy conglomeration of belching mills and terraced streets, peopled by cloth-capped, shuffling figures and matchstalk cats and dogs.

The reality is very different. Most of the mills have gone now and those that remain have been converted into upmarket apartments or shopping outlets. The name of L.S. Lowry, the artist who painted the industrial Lancashire of old, is now commemorated in the name of a cultural venue of international standing and daring design, which is just one of scores of innovative buildings that have sprung up on land left vacant by dead industries. The Greater Manchester of today is an area where tourist attractions range from ancient half-timbered halls and eighteenth-century weavers' villages to exciting new visitor centres, sporting venues and shopping destinations.

Leaving behind the former mill towns, we move north to Lancaster, the ancient capital of the county and a place with a rich heritage and a wonderful atmosphere. Using the city as a base, we explore Morecambe Bay, a region famed for its fabulous sunsets, where we discover a village with links to America's first president and a railway station that was the location for one of the most famous films of all time.

After travelling along the coast, we venture into the Lune Valley, one of the most beautiful and least spoilt valleys in England, where we discover tranquil river scenes, old-world bridges and a very photogenic castle.

Left: Part of the Oldham Panorama in Gallery Oldham

*Right:
Gallery
Oldham*

We then travel to the new city of Preston, where we visit the National Football Museum, before taking a trip along the Fylde Coast, which still ranks as England's foremost holiday playground. Moving inland, we explore the Forest of Bowland, an untouched land of round-topped moors and cosy villages, which is perhaps the best-kept beauty secret in England.

Changing our base to the ancient town of Clitheroe, we begin an exploration of the Ribble Valley, a region that the Queen has said she would choose as her retirement home in the highly unlikely event of her ever seeking one, and we circumnavigate Pendle Hill, a vast gritstone ridge that dominates the countryside for miles around and casts a spell on all who see it, not least because of its strong associations with the Lancashire Witches.

We travel to Liverpool, known throughout the world as the birthplace of the Beatles and as the home of the club that has won the European Cup more often than any other British side. The city is also known for its world-class museums and galleries, its great architectural legacy and its theatrical and musical pedigree, all of which contributed to its nomination as the European Capital of Culture for 2008.

Finally, we use Liverpool as a base for touring West Lancashire and the coast of Merseyside. We visit a theme park, a wildlife park and a safari park and we come across one hundred iron men standing on a vast beach, where they collectively form a sculpture called *Another Place*.

As this guide book seeks to demonstrate, it would be difficult to find another place which offers the variety, vibrancy and beauty that is contained in the county of Lancashire!

1. Manchester

In 1996, just two years before the signing of the Northern Ireland peace agreement, central Manchester was ripped apart by an IRA bomb that destroyed 75,000 square metres of retail and office space. Although the bomb caused no fatalities, it could have been the final nail in the coffin of a city that had been in decline ever since the demise of its cotton industry.

Above: The Albert Memorial and Manchester Town Hall in Albert Square

Below: Central Library and Town Hall extension, St Peter's Square, Manchester

Top Tips Manchester

- Take a tour of the great Victorian Town Hall, admire Waterhouse's masterpiece and see Ford Madox Brown's politically incorrect murals.

- Attend a concert in the fabulous auditorium of the Bridgewater Hall and listen to the celebrated Hallé Orchestra playing under the direction of their brilliant conductor Sir Mark Elder. Many of the concerts are designed for family audiences.

- Take the lift to Cloud 23, a bar on the 23rd floor of the Beetham Tower, and look through a porthole in the floor to the street far below, preferably before drinking a cocktail!

- Head for Deansgate and visit the cathedral-like John Rylands Library to inspect some of the oldest books and manuscripts in the world, before heading off to the Museum of Science and Industry and the Air and Space Museum, where children can have great fun with the interactive exhibits.

- Book a seat at the Royal Exchange Theatre and attend a production in an auditorium which looks like a space capsule that has been captured and locked in the largest indoor space in the North of England.

- Be seen shopping (or browsing) in Harvey Nichols and treat yourself, very occasionally, to a meal in the second-floor restaurant – the portions are small, but beautiful!

- Take the family for a slow spin on the Wheel of Manchester for an exciting bird's-eye view of the city (when the capsule has finally cleared the glass wall of Selfridges).

- Take the diagonal lift up the glass wall of Urbis and visit the exhibition rooms that are arranged like the ledges of a waterfall.

- Be sure to visit Manchester Cathedral to admire the widest nave in Britain, the sixteenth-century choir stalls and the modern stained glass.

- Spend time in Manchester Art Gallery, which has the country's best interactive gallery for children, as well as extensive exhibitions of work by L.S. Lowry, Adolphe Valette and the pre-Raphaelites.

However, thanks to the determination of the city council and the brilliant work of a task force that was set up immediately after the bomb went off, adversity was turned to advantage in the most spectacular fashion. The terrorist explosion became the catalyst for an explosion of new building that began with the stunning structures that were erected to renew the devastated area and then spread to all parts of the city. In no time at all, an exciting new Manchester began to rise phoenix-like from the ashes.

Just six years after the IRA attack, Manchester hosted a brilliantly successful Commonwealth Games, when the most positive image imaginable was beamed to a worldwide television audience of one billion people. One million people visited the city during the games and set in train an expansion in tourism that is seeing an annual increase of 300,000 visitors. Tourists are being drawn to the city by new world-class attractions such as Urbis, the Bridgewater Hall, The Lowry and the Imperial War Museum North, as well as two imaginatively revamped older attractions in the shape of Manchester Art Gallery and the John Rylands Library.

Thanks to massive inward investment, an insatiable demand for office space, a huge appetite for city-centre living and an ever-increasing need for new hotels to service a city that is now an internationally important business and tourist centre, scores of high-rise buildings have been erected throughout the central area and beyond. Like San Gimignano in the thirteenth century and New York in the twentieth century, twenty-first-century Manchester is expressing its vitality and confidence by reaching for the sky.

However, it would be wrong to diagnose the rash of daring new glass and steel structures as a plague that has wiped out the city's great Victorian heritage, because the best nineteenth-century warehouses and commercial buildings have been brought back to life as apartments or leisure and business spaces, while their exteriors have been restored to their full former glory.

The great Victorian Town Hall stands as a symbol of the days when Manchester was the cotton capital of the globe and an important centre for innovation in science, the arts and politics. Chetham's School of Music and Manchester Cathedral are impressive survivals of the medieval city that preceded the Industrial Revolution.

In fact, central Manchester probably has a greater concentration of architecturally significant buildings than any other urban area of comparable size. Within a rectangle measuring just three-quarters of a mile by one-quarter of a mile (1,200 metres by 400 metres), there are scores of landmark buildings from the three great ages of the city – its medieval origins, its Victorian heyday and its remarkable twenty-first-century renaissance.

Opposite page: The Touchstone outside the Bridgewater Hall

1. Manchester

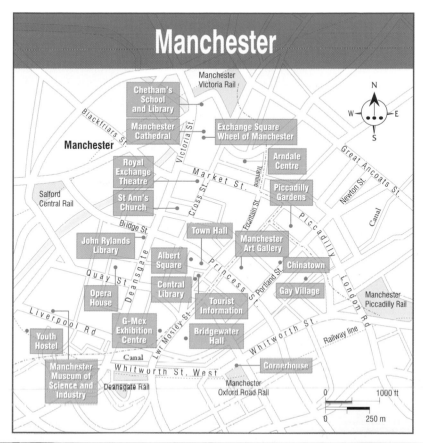

Manchester

- Chetham's School and Library
- Manchester Victoria Rail
- Manchester Cathedral
- Exchange Square Wheel of Manchester
- Arndale Centre
- Royal Exchange Theatre
- St Ann's Church
- Piccadilly Gardens
- John Rylands Library
- Town Hall
- Manchester Art Gallery
- Chinatown
- Albert Square
- Central Library
- Opera House
- Tourist Information
- Gay Village
- Manchester Piccadilly Rail
- G-Mex Exhibition Centre
- Bridgewater Hall
- Youth Hostel
- Manchester Museum of Science and Industry
- Cornerhouse
- Manchester Oxford Road Rail

Blackfriars St — Victoria St — Market St. — Great Ancoats St. — Newton St. — Canal — Cross St. — Fountain St. — Piccadilly — Bridge St. — Quay St — Deansgate — Princess St — Portland St. — London Rd — Liverpool Rd — Lwr Mosley St. — Whitworth St. — Railway line — Canal — Whitworth St. West — Deansgate Rail

Salford Central Rail

0 — 1000 ft
0 — 250 m

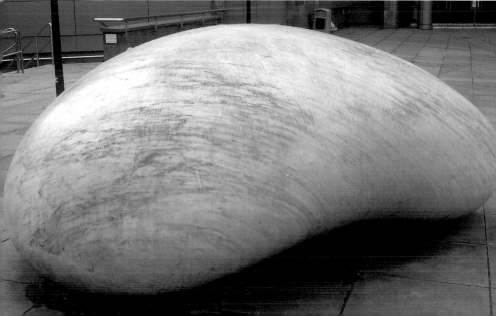

A Walking Tour of the City

Albert Square and the Town Hall

Our tour begins in **Albert Square**, a Victorian civic space that contains a number of significant monuments and ranks in magnificence alongside Europe's great medieval squares.

The elaborate, canopied **Albert Memorial** represents the patronage that Queen Victoria's consort gave to industry, commerce and the arts. It was erected in 1867, several years before its twin in London. One of the most important statues in the square depicts John Bright, the radical politician who was a champion of free trade and campaigned for the abolition of the Corn Laws.

Albert Square is overlooked by the clock tower and the soaring Gothic pinnacles and turrets of the **Town Hall**, Alfred Waterhouse's masterpiece and a fitting expression of Victorian Manchester's civic pride. The building is adorned with statues of the great and the good, including Edward III, who is credited with laying the foundations of Manchester's trade by introducing Flemish weavers to England; Thomas Gresley, who granted the city its first charter in 1301; and Humphrey Chetham, who founded Chetham's Hospital and Library.

The clock tower is 280ft (85m) high and crowned by a ball with 29 spikes. Every Christmas it is decorated with a huge effigy of Father Christmas and is the centrepiece of illuminations that attract families from miles around.

A tour of the building begins at the main entrance, which is framed by statues of Salford-born James Joule,

Commemoration of the historic meeting of Rolls and Royce at the Midland Hotel

The Beetham Tower from Deansgate

Dappled light on the gothic frontage of the John Rylands Library

who gave his name to a unit of energy, and John Dalton, who taught mathematics and philosophy in Manchester and was the first scientist to suggest that all matter is composed of atoms. The **Great Hall,** on the first floor, is decorated with twelve murals by the celebrated pre-Raphaelite artist Ford Madox Brown.

Although the paintings supposedly represent the history of Manchester, they are based on a rather liberal interpretation of historical facts and borrow freely from events that took place elsewhere. They also show a very blatant disregard for political correctness. For example, one painting shows

an apprentice eyeing up his master's daughter, another features a young boy casually kicking a Nubian slave, while a depiction of the opening of the Bridgewater Canal is dominated by a pair of very plump twin babies.

The Town Hall is linked by a flyover to the **Town Hall Extension.** Far from being an add-on, this is a brilliant building in its own right. Designed by Vincent Harris in the 1930s, it is a very clever architectural link between the Gothic Town Hall and the Classical **Central Library**. A fine curved walkway between the Extension and the Library provides spectacular views of the two buildings.

St Peter's Square and Lower Mosley Street

The **Central Library,** which was also designed by Vincent Harris, was opened in 1934 as the largest municipal library in Britain. The huge circular reading room on the first floor resembles that in the British Museum and the **Library Theatre** in the basement is a venue for some of the very best contemporary productions.

In the centre of the square is a **Cenotaph**, which was erected on the site of the old St Peter's Church. Between the cenotaph and the library there are boarding platforms for the trams that run through the heart of the city. Close to the **Tourist Information Centre**, there is a statue that commemorates Manchester's status as the world's first nuclear-free city.

The square is overlooked from its southern side by the **Midland Hotel**, a monumental structure faced in polished granite and Burmantofts faience. It was built in 1903 by the Midland Railway Company as an architectural balance for the Midland Grand Hotel, St Pancras at the London end of the railway line.

In May 1904, Henry Edmunds brought the luxury-car dealer Charles Rolls to the hotel and introduced him to the brilliant automotive engineer Henry Royce. Their meeting resulted in the creation of a company that would produce and market the Rolls-Royce, which established a reputation as 'the finest motor car in the world'. The historic encounter is commemorated by a mural in the foyer of the hotel.

When the Midland Hotel was first built it was linked by a passageway to the Midland Railway's enormous station. The passageway no longer exists and the huge station has been converted into the **G-Mex Exhibition Centre**, part of the Manchester Central Convention Complex, which is a venue for events of national importance, including party conferences.

One side of the exhibition centre flanks Lower Mosley Street, which is also the site of the **Bridgewater Hall**, a state-of-the-art home for the famous Hallé Orchestra, Britain's oldest symphony orchestra, which was founded in 1858 by Sir Charles Hallé. The building, which has a magnificent 2,000-seater auditorium, fronts Barbirolli Square, where there is a statue to Sir John Barbirolli, the Hallé's most famous conductor, as well as Kan Yasuda's super-smooth, tactile sculpture, which is known as the **Touchstone**.

Sir Mark Elder, the current musical director of the orchestra, has not only ensured that the Hallé's concerts are of the very highest quality, but has also designed many of them to appeal to children.

Peter St., Oxford St., and Oxford Rd.

The long road running south from St Peter's Square is Oxford Street, which then becomes Oxford Road. Its buildings include the **Palace Theatre**, which is one of the best-equipped theatres outside London and is the venue for many regional premieres, and the **Cornerhouse,** Manchester's centre for contemporary visual art and film.

The Cornerhouse is followed by the university quarter, which includes the Manchester Museum and the Whitworth Gallery. The **Manchester Museum** has one of the largest collections of ancient Egyptian artefacts in the UK, as well as one million botanical specimens and a vivarium containing frogs, amphibians and other reptiles. The **Whitworth Gallery** has a very fine display of art, including a large space devoted to contemporary art, as well as an internationally important collection of wallpapers and textiles.

The road running north-west from St Peter's Square is Peter Street, which is dominated by the **Free Trade Hall**, the former home of the Hallé and now converted into the Radisson Hotel. A plaque on the wall indicates that the building is close to St Peter's Field, where the **Peterloo Massacre** took place on 16 August 1819, when armed cavalry charged a gathering of 60,000 pro-democracy reformers. The result was 11 deaths and over 500 serious injuries.

After crossing Deansgate, St Peter's Street becomes Quay Street, which is the location for the **Opera House**, a 1,920-seater theatre that stages musicals, ballet, concerts and pantomimes.

Deansgate

The long road known as Deansgate has a number of architecturally significant buildings, including **Sunlight House**, Manchester's first skyscraper, which was built in 1931 in the 'step-back' style of 1930s' New York by Joe Sunlight, a flamboyant entrepreneur with a name to match.

Clearly visible in the southern reaches of Deansgate is the **Beetham Tower,** a 47-storey skyscraper, which was completed in 2006 and designed by Ian Simpson, who lives on the 47th floor in a penthouse surrounded by olive trees that were shipped in by helicopter. The first 23 floors are occupied by the Hilton Hotel, while the remaining 24 floors, which cantilever out over the hotel in spectacular fashion, are given over to apartments.

On the 23rd floor of the tower there is a bar known as Cloud 23, which has expansive views towards the Peak District in the east and Snowdonia in the south. Two glass portholes, which are set in the floor, provide a dizzy bird's-eye-view of the street far below – it is advisable to take in the view before you have a drink! A notable feature of the Beetham Tower is a huge vane on its summit, which had to be dampened when the building first opened because windy conditions caused it to emit a middle C note that was so loud that it disturbed actors on the set of *Coronation Street* in the nearby Granada Studios!

This end of Deansgate leads to **Castlefield**, where the **Bridgewater Canal,** the world's first commercial canal, enters the city. Once a major industrial area, it is now given over to apartments, bars, waterside pubs and an outdoor arena. The area is also home to the **Manchester Museum of Science and Industry** and an **Air and Space Museum,** two interactive exhibition spaces that appeal to visitors of all ages.

Retracing our steps up Deansgate towards the city centre, we come to **Spinningfields**, a complex of high-rise office, residential and leisure developments, which covers 6 acres (2.5 hectares) between Deansgate and

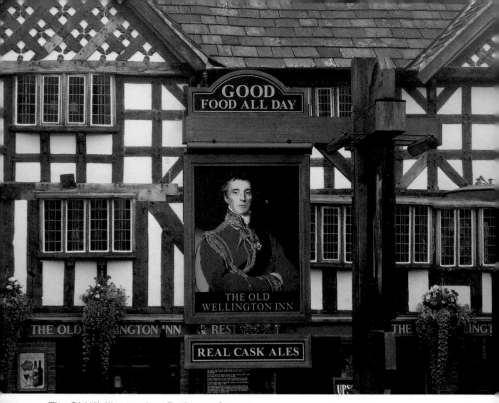

The Old Wellington Inn, Exchange Square

Bridge Street, where the floors of the new **Civil Justice Centre** jut out like the partially-opened drawers of a huge filing cabinet.

The ornate Gothic building that stands next to the Deansgate frontage of Spinningfields is the **John Rylands Library,** which was founded by Enriqueta Rylands as a memorial to her husband, who was Manchester's first cotton millionaire. The building, which is now approached via an all-glass entrance hall, is home to one of the world's great collections of books and manuscripts. Exhibits include Western and Oriental manuscripts dating back to the third millennium BC; an extract from Homer's *Odyssey* copied out by a schoolboy in ancient Greece; and all but one of the 15 incunable editions of Dante's *Divine Comedy*. It is impos-

sible not to feel deep reverence for these ancient works, especially as they are displayed in rooms that resemble chapels and cloisters. In fact, the great reading room of the library is like the nave of a Gothic cathedral.

Beyond the junction of Bridge Street and John Dalton Street, Deansgate is crossed by King Street, which has some of the trendiest shops in Manchester. Deansgate itself has a huge branch of Waterstone's, some excellent eating places, including the Living Room, founded by former Australian soap star Tim Bacon, and the former Kendal's department store, now rebranded as a House of Fraser, which is located in a monumental 1930s building with echoes of the type of Germanic styling pioneered by Messel.

Above: Royal Exchange Theatre

Right: Barton Arcade

Below: The Wheel of Manchester

St Ann's Square

A right turn opposite the House of Fraser leads to St Ann's Square, which has yet more smart shops and is the venue for excellent Continental Markets. The square is overlooked by **St Ann's Church**, a pink-sandstone, eighteenth-century building with a fine galleried interior. It is open daily and houses many events.

The **Royal Exchange,** at the opposite end of the square, was once the trading room for almost all the world's cotton business; it now houses the **Royal Exchange Theatre**, whose architecture is as brilliant as its productions. Its hi-tech auditorium, which looks like Neil Armstrong's moonlander capsule, is suspended in the largest indoor space in the north of England.

Barton Arcade, which runs off Deansgate, is a spectacular galleried, glass-roofed Victorian shopping arcade and home to several classy boutiques.

Exchange Square and the Cathedral Quarter

A left turn from the Royal Exchange leads to the head of Deansgate, where the giant, all-glass, wedge-shaped apartment block known as **No.1 Deansgate** is an icon of the twenty-first century city and an introduction to one of Manchester's most vibrant new districts. This area contains the **Harvey Nichols Store**, with its fabulous second-floor restaurant, and is focused on **Exchange Square,** where a former corn exchange

and an old printworks have been imaginatively converted into shopping and entertainment complexes.

The centre of the square is dominated by the **Wheel of Manchester**, a huge ferris wheel that provides spectacular views over the city – once the rotation has cleared the glass facade of the Selfridges/Marks and Spencer building. Although Exchange Square is the city's newest space, it is flanked by one of Manchester's oldest buildings, the half-timbered **Old Shambles**, containing the Wellington Inn and Sinclair's Oyster Bar.

The best of the old is overlooked by the best of the new in the form of **Urbis**, another all-glass wedge designed by Ian Simpson, which houses a series of exhibition spaces that cascade down the building like the ledges of a waterfall. The series of changing exhibitions includes shows devoted to many and varied aspects of life for young and old in twenty-first-century cities such as Manchester.

There are some fine survivals from pre-Industrial Revolution Manchester in the area immediately north of Exchange Square, where we find **Chetham's School and Library,** founded in 1653 by Humphrey Chetham. The school is a centre of excellence for students of music and the library is the oldest lending library in the English-speaking world. A four-sided desk in an alcove was regularly used as a base for study by Karl Marx and Friedrich Engels.

Chetham's School stands close to **Manchester Cathedral**, which has the widest nave in Britain, fine sixteenth-century choir stalls and some good modern stained glass that was installed to replace windows that were shattered by bombs in the Second World War.

The Arndale Centre, Market Street and Piccadilly Gardens

A return to Exchange Square brings us face-to-face with a giant Next store and the entrance to the **Arndale Centre,** which is the largest city-centre indoor shopping mall in Europe, with 130,000 square metres of retail space. The other main entrance to the centre is on Market Street, one of Manchester's main shopping streets, where there are large department stores, including Debenhams, Marks and Spencer and Primark.

A walk along Market Street leads to **Piccadilly Gardens**, another of Manchester's great civic spaces. The square is overlooked by a trio of sixties buildings that were much derided as brutalist monstrosities but are now listed as important examples of the monumental concrete architecture of the period. The square itself has been remodelled since the Millennium and adorned with a curved concrete pavilion and a pedestrian footway that is raised above a pool with dancing fountains.

The Gay Village and Chinatown

In the south-east corner of Piccadilly Gardens, Portland Street leads to **Chinatown,** which has an Imperial Chinese Archway and many outlets for Chinese food. Aytoun Street leads to the **Gay Village**, which has a look of Amsterdam with its plethora of bars and restaurants set alongside the Rochdale Canal.

The Art Gallery

A walk down Mosley Street, to the south of Piccadilly, brings us to **Manchester Art Gallery**, home to one of the finest collections of pre-Raphaelite art in the world. The exhibition spaces, which were originally confined to two classical buildings designed by Sir Charles Barry, have now been greatly expanded by the addition of an extension by Sir Michael Hopkins. They include a large craft and design gallery, a vast space devoted to modern art, a room dedicated to Lowry and his mentor Adolphe Valette, and a fabulous interactive children's gallery, where children can bring paintings to life and create their own works of art. This space is hugely popular with young visitors.

Although Hopkins' extension to the gallery is uncompromisingly modern in design, it mirrors one of Barry's original buildings in shape and size. This juxtaposition of old and new is a fitting finale to a tour that has taken in an eclectic mix of architectural masterpieces from the last half-millennium, all of which combine to form the visually exciting whole that is central Manchester.

The Town Hall, where we began our walk, is just a block away.

Above: Urbis   *Below: Statue of Humphrey Chetham in Manchester Cathedral*

Above: The Arndale Centre   *Below: China Town, Manchester*

Places to Visit Manchester

Air and Space Museum and Museum of Science and Industry

Castlefield
☎ 0161 832 2244
Open: every day except 24–26 Dec and 1 Jan; 10am–5pm

Chetham's Library

Long Millgate
☎ 0161 834 7961
Open by appointment: Mon to Fri, except Bank and Public Holidays 9am–12.30pm; 1.30pm–4.30pm

Cornerhouse

Oxford Street
☎ 0161 200 1500
Galleries open: Tue–Sat 11am–6pm; Thu late night to 8pm; Sun 2pm–6pm

John Rylands Library

Deansgate
☎ 0161 275 3716
Open: Mon to Sat 10am–5pm; Sun 12pm–5pm
Closed: Good Friday, Easter Sunday and between Christmas and New Year

Manchester Art Gallery

Mosley Street
☎ 0161 235 8888
Open: Tue to Sun and Bank Holiday Mondays: 10am to 5pm
Closed: Mon (except Bank Holidays); Good Friday; 24–26 Dec; New Year's Eve; New Year's Day

Manchester Museum

Oxford Road
☎ 0161 275 2634
Open: Mon. Sun and Bank Holidays 11am–4pm; Tue to Sat 10am–5pm

Manchester Town Hall

Albert Square
For guided Blue Badge Tours, contact Manchester Visitor Centre
☎ 0871 222 8223

Urbis

Cathedral Gardens
☎ 0161 605 8200
Open: Tue–Sun 10am–6pm

Wheel of Manchester

Exchange Square
☎ 0161 831 9918
Open: Sun to Thu 10am–11pm; Fri 10am–12 midnight; Sat 9am–12 midnight.
Christmas Eve 9am–6pm; closed Christmas Day; Boxing Day 10am–7pm.
New Year's Eve 10am–2am; New Year's Day 12pm–6pm

Whitworth Gallery

Oxford Road
☎ 01273 623266
Open: Mon Sat 10am–5pm; Sun 12pm–4pm

THEATRES, CONCERT HALLS

To discover what's on at all the Manchester theatres and concert halls, visit www. manchestertheatres.com

HOTELS

There are well over 100 hotels in the Manchester area, including three five-star hotels (Lowry Hotel, Radisson Edwardian, Blue Rainbow ApartHotel) and 47 four-star hotels. For visitors planning an overnight stay, the best bet is to consult the internet.

YOUTH HOSTEL

Manchester

Potato Wharf
Castlefields
M3 4NB
☎ 0870 770 5950

RESTAURANTS

There are some 200 restaurants in the city, many of which are excellent. Some of the best include: Grado on New York Street; 110 in the Circus Casino on Portland Street; Michael Caine's in the Abode Hotel, Piccadilly; Choice on Castle Quay; the Grill in the Alley, just off Deansgate; Chaophraya in Chapel Walks; Petit Blanc, just off King Street, and Harvey Nichols' Second Floor Restaurant on New Cathedral Street.

SHOPPING

Manchester is a paradise for shoppers. Market Street includes Primark, Debenhams, Marks and Spencer and the vast Arndale Centre; Deansgate includes the House of Fraser; King Street, St Ann's Square and the surrounding arcades contain boutique shops; Exchange Square includes Next, Selfridges and the Triangle shopping centre.

TOURIST INFORMATION CENTRE

Town Hall Extension
☎ 0871 222 8223

2. Ten Highlights of Greater Manchester

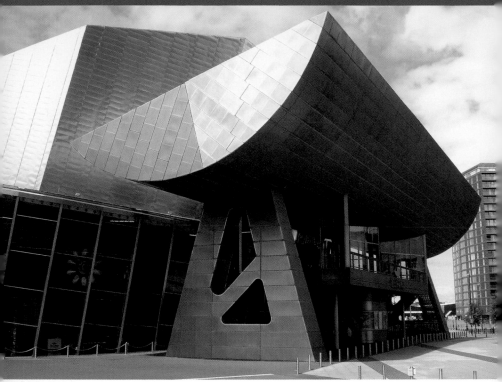

When the new Metropolitan County of Greater Manchester was created in 1974, the city was allowed to swallow up great chunks of land from the old counties of Lancashire, Cheshire and Yorkshire.

As this book is a guide to the Lancashire of the popular imagination, rather than the one drawn up by bureaucrats in Whitehall, we'll allow the southern part of this sprawling metropolitan county of two and a half million people to be counted as Cheshire, but we'll claim for Lancashire all those areas to the north of a line of latitude running through the centre of Manchester.

In the early eighteenth century, much of this area was a rural land populated by moorland farmers and home-weavers. A century later, great swathes of countryside had been transformed into a conglomeration of densely populated mill towns, with terrace upon terrace of workers' houses standing in the shadow of huge mills dedicated to cotton processing. In 1910, the town of Oldham alone had over 250 mills.

The most impressive factories from the industrial age have been conserved and converted into apartment blocks or

retail outlets. In some cases, their machinery has been salvaged and brought back to working order as evidence of the engineering skill of our forebears.

In many of the areas where factories and industrial installations have been removed, the land has been redeveloped for residential, retail, cultural or leisure use, often in the most innovative and spectacular fashion. Similarly, industrial waterways from the Canal Age have been reborn as routes for pleasure craft.

Weavers' villages from the pre-factory days have become desirable places of residence, as well as favoured spots for artists and craftspeople to set up their studios. Timber-framed country houses from even earlier times have bent and bowed over the centuries, but they have never broken. They survive as treasured examples of Lancashire's elaborate black-and-white style of architecture.

The people of the mill towns also remained unbroken through many periods of hardship, which began with the Cotton Famine of the 1860s, when the American Civil War brought about an embargo on the export of raw cotton, through the years of the Great Depression and fierce competition from Indian and Japanese producers, to the terminal decline of the industry during the post-war years.

Impoverished workers survived these hard times by buying cheap, wholesome food from the market stalls of local suppliers and using it to develop their own dishes, which are now prized as elements in gourmet recipes. Even today, huge stall markets are one of the most characteristic features of the former mill towns.

Our clockwise tour around the northern arc of Greater Manchester will embrace all these fascinating and varied elements from Lancashire's past and present. We begin our journey at **Salford Quays**, just four miles (6.5km) west of Manchester's city centre.

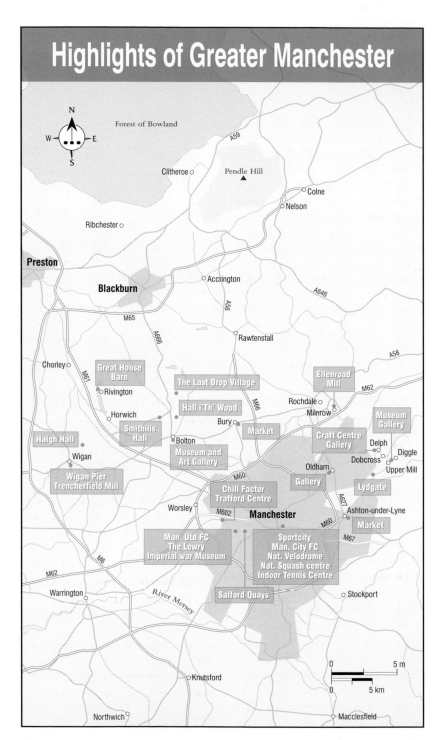

Highlights of Greater Manchester

Salford Quays

The metamorphosis of Manchester from a city in decline into a vibrant Barcelona of the North is amazing enough, but the transformation of Salford Quays from a dead port on the Manchester Ship Canal into one of the most spectacular cultural, residential and business quarters in Europe is even more staggering. A wasteland has become a brand new city of glass towers set alongside **The Lowry**, a great arts centre named after the artist who painted the industrial Salford that is long gone.

The centre, which was designed by Michael Wilford, sits alongside the canal like a great liner. Visitors enter the building under a huge projecting canopy, which is seen as intimidating by some, but welcoming by others and unforgettable by all. Within the many-layered, brightly coloured interior, there are galleries, theatres, restaurants, cafés and bookshops.

Several spaces are devoted to an enormous collection of paintings and drawings by **L.S. Lowry**, whose work is immensely appealing to young and old. The **Lyric Theatre** combines an intimate auditorium with one of the biggest stages outside London, which allows it to attract large-scale productions that could not be staged elsewhere, while the **Quays Theatre** has highly flexible stage and seating arrangements.

Facing The Lowry, there is a large **Designer Outlet**, which forms the base of a towering apartment block. Across the canal, there stands the **Imperial War Museum North,** one of the world's most innovative buildings. Designed by the brilliant architect Daniel Libeskind, its three-part form represents a globe that has been shattered by conflict and reconstructed into three shards, representing war at sea, on the land and in the air.

The Water Shard, which contains a restaurant, projects over the Manchester Ship Canal; the Earth Shard not only contains all the museum's exhibits but also becomes a giant cinema auditorium at regular intervals, when very moving images of the devastating effects of war are projected onto all four walls. The Air Shard has a viewing platform 25 metres above the ground, from where visitors can look right along the canal to Manchester's city centre, as though they were bomber pilots flying in to wreak havoc on the city. Far from being a museum that celebrates war, this is a museum that graphically exposes the effects of war and the reality of life in a theatre of conflict.

A little further along the south bank of the canal, there is a theatre for battles of a very different sort. **Old Trafford** is the home of Manchester United, one of the world's richest and most successful football clubs. Tickets for matches are hard to come by, but tours can be made of the ground, popularly known as the Theatre of Dreams. The Manchester United Museum charts the glorious, but often turbulent, history of the club, including its rise from the ashes of the Munich Air Disaster of 1958, when almost an entire team was wiped out. To the delight of young visitors, there is also ample and very graphic coverage of the team's current superstars.

The Trafford Centre

With 230 stores, a 20-screen cinema and more than 60 restaurants, bars and cafés, the **Trafford Centre** is a truly enormous out-of-town shopping destination. Situated 4.5 miles (7km) west of the city centre and close to the M60, the centre is an unmistakable landmark on Manchester's orbital motorway.

Its fake classical statues, mock-Egyptian temples and preposterous domes are not to everyone's taste, but for shopaholics this is as close to heaven as you can get, even though the Trafford Centre's version of heaven is a depiction of the sky painted on the inside of the complex's biggest dome. Regular tea dances are held in the vast food court, which is designed like the deck of a great ocean liner.

Close by the Trafford Centre, there is a gargantuan inclined plane, which houses **Chill Factor**, the biggest indoor ski centre in the country. Facilities include three interconnected snow slopes to cater for different levels of ability, as well as a toboggan run, an indoor skateboard park and a children's play area.

The M60 motorway swings northwards from the Trafford Centre to the village of Worsley.

Worsley

In 1748, when Francis Egerton inherited the **Worsley** estates and became the Third Duke of Bridgewater, he was told by his land agent, John Gilbert, that he was sitting on a gold mine; or, to be more precise, a rich seam of coal.

The Duke commissioned James Brindley to build the world's first commercial canal to transport the coal to Manchester, while Gilbert designed a series of underground channels to connect with the canal and allow the boats to be loaded directly at the coalface.

The entrance to the canals, which stretched for 42 miles, can still be seen at Worsley Delph. Worsley Green, which was once covered by the workshops of boat-builders, nail-makers and wheelwrights, is now a huge unspoilt village green surrounded by black-and-white houses built by the Duke and his successors. As a result, the former industrial centre looks like an archetypal old-world English village.

Although the canal is still tinted orange by iron deposits from the old

Bridgewater Canal at Worsley

Above: Wigan – entrance to the Galleries

mine workings, it is now a popular haunt for narrowboat enthusiasts, not least because the good mooring facilities give easy access to the many excellent restaurants in the picturesque village.

The **Church of St Mark** was designed by the distinguished architect George Gilbert Scott. It has a tall spire that is well known to travellers on the M60 motorway, which runs close by the building, and it has a clock with a very unusual feature. The timepiece was once sited on the village green, where its one o'clock bell summoned workers back to work after their lunch break. When the Canal Duke realised that some workers were arriving late for their shift on the pretext that they couldn't hear the single chime above the noise of the machinery, he had the mechanism altered so that it would chime 13 times at one o'clock!

The Worsley area has no fewer than four golf courses. According to rumour, it will soon have a horse-racing track too.

A dozen miles (20km) to the west of Worsley lies Wigan.

Wigan

Thanks to its use as a musical joke by George Formby Senior and its inclusion in the title of George Orwell's book about the terrible living conditions of England's working poor, **Wigan Pier** evokes an image that is the very antithesis of the picture of a seaside resort with a real pier.

However, do not be misled. **Wigan** includes much more positive assets than its legendary old industrial jetty. If shopping is the new rock 'n' roll, Wigan is one of the most swinging towns in the country. Alongside independent shops, specialist outlets, indoor and outdoor markets and chain stores, there are enough top designer outlets to make Wigan one of the 'coolest' destinations in the North West.

Shopping in Wigan is all the more pleasurable because so much of it is undercover. Ever since Makinson's arcade was constructed in Edwardian times, shopping arcades have been a feature of the central area. The latest addition is the Grand Arcade, a glass-topped mall with 425,000 square feet of retail space and cafés.

The centre contains a heritage board and a statue of George Formby (Junior), and shoppers in Marks and Spencer are regularly entertained by Jim Taylor at the piano. And that fabled area around Wigan Pier is currently undergoing conversion into a new residential, commercial, leisure and retail area centred on Trencherfield Mill, where the steam engine is being retained as a working exhibit.

Just outside Wigan, there is a large mansion known as **Haigh Hall**. Surrounded by a country park and golf course, it has a stables block that houses a popular tea room, where Mrs Dowson's famous ice cream is on sale. This delicious product is based on the flavours of exotic fruits that were once grown in the greenhouses of the hall.

Bolton is ten miles (16km) north-east of Wigan.

Bolton and the West Pennines

Bolton has a very impressive town centre with a fine shopping area, an art gallery with excellent examples of twentieth-century drawings, a museum with an extensive Egyptology section, a grand central square and an impressive Town Hall that looks uncannily like the great Victorian town hall across the Pennines in Leeds.

The town also has a glorious West Pennine hinterland dotted with half-timbered country houses and charming villages. **Hall i' th' Wood** is a fifteenth-century half-timbered hall that was purchased and restored in 1902 by William Hesketh Lever, the founder of Lever Brothers and a former mayor of Bolton. The house, which was once the home of Samuel Crompton, inventor of

George Formby, Wigan

the spinning mule, contains a museum with a mix of changing and permanent exhibitions.

Smithills Hall, which is located a few miles to the west, is a large manor house with architectural elements from the Medieval, Tudor and Arts and Crafts periods. The hall is the centrepiece of a large country park, which includes an open farm, and the coach house has a fine restaurant where themed nights are often held.

The Last Drop Village stands on the fringe of the moors to the north of Bolton. Its picturesque high street contains jewellers, a children's bookshop, a fine art and sculpture gallery, a shop selling traditional toys, a tea shop, a restaurant and a pub.

It comes as a surprise to discover that this old-world village was actually created in the sixties by Carlton Walker, who renovated and converted a group of eighteenth- and nineteenth-century farm buildings. Even more surprisingly, the whole complex is situated within the grounds of a hotel, which has some of its suites above the shops in the village street.

And why is it called the Last Drop Village? One theory has it that the name was suggested by Carlton Walker's friends, who offered him the last drop of a bottle of wine during a meal to celebrate the completion of building work. Another version has Mrs Walker telling her husband at the celebration meal that his spending on the project had taken the last drop of their money!

A much more genuine old village is to be found straddled along a causeway between the high moors and a vast man-made lake. This is the village of **Rivington**, which has a sixteenth-century parish church and a sloping village green complete with a set of stocks.

Great House Barn, which stands close to the reservoir, is a huge Scandinavian-style structure, which has a massive oak-timbered roof that is said to date from Saxon times. It now accommodates a popular café and gift shop. The adjacent Great House Farm houses an information centre and there is a picnic area between the barn and the reservoir.

An avenue of beech trees leads to an almost identical barn, which stands next to **Rivington Hall**, an impressive Georgian mansion that was restored by soap-maker William Lever, who also built a replica of Liverpool Castle on a bluff overlooking the lake. **Rivington Pike**, on a 1,191ft (363m) summit above the village, was built in 1733 on a former beacon site. Thousands of Lancastrians walk to the summit on Good Friday and hundreds of athletes race to the top on Easter Sunday.

Bury is located six miles (10km) southeast of Bolton and Ashton-under-Lyne is a further 14 miles (22km) in the same direction.

Bury and Ashton-Under-Lyne markets

While stall markets are immensely popular in mainland Europe, they have gone into a sad decline in most of Britain. But not so in Lancashire! Among the many large indoor and

Above left: Village Green, Rivington Above right: Timber framing at Smithills Hall

outdoor markets in the former mill towns, those at **Bury** and **Ashton-under-Lyne** stand out as the biggest and the best. With 370 stalls, 200,000 square feet of selling area, bargains galore and a cast of colourful stallholders, Bury Market attracts 250,000 visitors per week. It has been voted a 'Top Ten UK Food Market'.

In 2004, the interior of Ashton-under-Lyne's Market Hall was destroyed by a devastating fire. Fortunately, the historic shell of the building survived and now encases the completely rebuilt interior, which has a spectacular new glass roof designed with subtle twists and turns that allow it to fit the awkward pentagonal shape of the Victorian shell. The huge public square in front of the indoor market contains 143 outdoor stalls and is backed by two modern shopping precincts, one of which has recently undergone a revamp that has included the addition of a spectacular new entranceway. Beyond the precincts, there is a huge

box-like building that houses a vast IKEA store.

Milnrow is ten miles (16km) north of Ashton-under-Lyne

Milnrow and Hollingworth Lake

Victoria and Alexandra are the world's largest steam cotton mill engines. First installed in Milnrow's **Ellenroad Mill** in 1892, they were saved, along with the factory's boiler house, engine house and chimney, and restored to working order when the mill was demolished in 1982. Steam days are held each month, when the machines are fired up and members of the public are invited to attend an audience with these two queens of steam.

At the point where the former mill town gives way to high moors, there is a **Soccer Village**, complete with a restaurant called the **Top Tier**. Another hilltop building on the opposite side

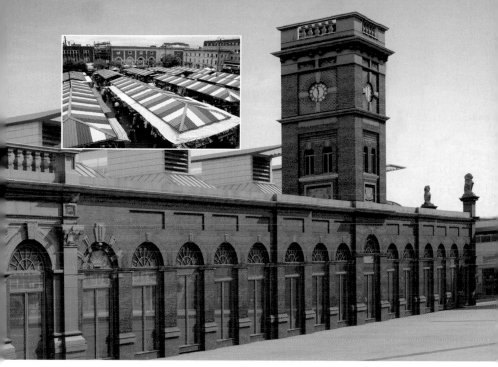

Above: The restored Market Hall, Ashton-Under-Lyne and (inset) Ashton Market

Above: The Square in the village of Dobcross

of the road accommodates the **Bella Vista,** a pizzeria and restaurant, which, as its name implies, commands spectacular views.

The location of Bella Vista's sister restaurant, **The Wine Press,** is very different, but equally splendid. It stands on the shore of nearby **Hollingworth Lake,** a very popular beauty spot that was once known as the 'Weavers' Seaside'. It is said that Captain Webb trained on the lake to prepare for his famous swim across the English Channel.

Oldham is 6 miles (10km) south of Milnrow

Oldham

In its industrial heyday, Oldham had over 250 mills, which operated night and day. The townscape of Victorian Oldham is graphically illustrated in the **Oldham Panorama,** made up of nine photographs taken during Wakes Week in 1876, when the mills had shut down for the annual holiday. Thanks to a rare smoke-free interlude, the photographer had a clear view of the entire town, which was an unhealthy jumble of mean terraces and huge factories.

This remarkable illustration occupies the entire wall of a link-corridor in **Gallery Oldham,** the most spectacular building in the new town that has arisen since the decline of the cotton industry. The building, which has two huge semi-circular glass observation platforms on its top floor, occupies a site where factories once belched out so much smoke that the fine view of the moors that can now be enjoyed was almost obliterated. Gallery Oldham stages an excellent series of changing exhibitions by artists

of local and national importance.

Oldham's new cultural credentials are also in evidence in **The Spindles** shopping mall, where Brian Clarke's stained-glass roof takes the form of a tribute to Oldham-born composer Sir William Walton – look out for musical references among the colourful motifs!

Oldham has another claim to fame: it is the birthplace of **Sarsaparilla,** once the favourite tipple of the Temperance Movement. At one time there were over 20 herbalist shops-cum-temperance bars in Oldham. One of these was owned by Joe Mawson, a milkman-turned-herbalist, whose bar became known for its Sarsaparilla 'beer'.

Sarsaparilla is a South American root bark, which can supposedly cure rheumatism, skin disorders and sexual impotence. Joe hit upon the idea of adding ginger and liquorice to his brew and selling the drink as a pleasant tonic. Although his temperance bar closed in 1963, he established a firm in Bacup to produce Sarsaparilla, which remains a popular drink to this day.

Saddleworth is six miles (10km) north-east of Oldham

Saddleworth

Writing about the various settlements that make up **Saddleworth,** Glyn Hughes described them as villages that are 'isolated in a foreign country, regarding themselves as Yorkshire villages holding out against over-spilling industrial Lancashire'.

Saddleworth managed to hold out until the boundary changes of 1974, when all the villages were swallowed up by Greater Manchester. However, the refusal of many people to accept their new status as Lancastrians is reflected in the sign at the entrance to the excellent **Saddleworth Museum**. It reads: 'The story of a Yorkshire community on the Lancashire side of the Pennines.'

The museum traces the evolution of a group of home-weaving settlements into places where textiles were manufactured in large mills. Evidence of home-weaving is still apparent in the upper storeys of the cottages, where the weaving was carried out in rooms that were lit by very wide windows subdivided by many mullions.

These wide upper windows are particularly apparent in the village of **Dobcross**, where some of the top-floor windows of the three-storey cottages are subdivided by as many as a dozen mullions. The village, which clings to a hillside below a pretty cobbled square, has something of the look of an Italian hill village – even its church is Italianate!

By way of contrast, **Delph** snuggles in a deep valley. Several of its old weavers' cottages have outside stairways known as 'takin' in steps', which were used to deliver cloth. A building dated 1769 now houses Mary Isherwood's fish and chip shop, which must rank as one of England's most picturesque chippies; other cottages have been converted into trendy restaurants. An old Co-op building now accommodates the **Saddleworth Crafts Co-operative**, which was founded by John McCombs, who has dedicated his life to producing superb paintings of Delph and its surroundings. He has a permanent exhibition in the building.

Art is also well represented in the **Millyard Gallery** in **Uppermill**, which not only features work by the large colony of local artists, but also paintings and prints by some of the country's leading painters. Uppermill's main street has much to offer the visitor, because it is lined with craft shops, designer shops and café bars.

The neighbouring village of **Diggle** is the starting point of the **Huddersfield Narrow Canal**, a 3.25-mile (5km) tunnel that was opened in 1810 after 17 years of boring through the Pennines. Hailed as the highest, longest and deepest canal tunnel in Britain, its profitable days came to an end with the opening of the Standedge railway tunnel, just 38 years later. Eventually the canal route closed, but it was reopened for pleasure craft in 2001.

The story of the construction and use of the Standedge Tunnel, which includes heroic efforts, mortal blows and renewed glory, is told in the most entertaining fashion on a path leading to the tunnel entrance. Slabs inscribed with descriptions of key events in the tunnel's history are laid out like a board game and a spinning dice is provided. Each triumph merits a move forward; each disaster a move back!

There are two other musts for visitors to Saddleworth: **Newbank Garden Centre**, on the road between Delph and Dobcross; and the **White Hart** in the lofty Saddleworth village of **Lydgate**. Until recent years, the White Hart was a run-down pub, where three of the locals were the inspiration for Compo, Clegg and Blamire in the television series *Last of the Summer Wine*. It has now been transformed into a superb hotel and restaurant, where the food is so good that one critic commented: 'Forget sexy food; this is pornographic.'

Sportcity is 12 miles (19km) south-west of Saddleworth

Sportcity

Our semicircular tour ends at **Sportcity** in East Manchester. Developed for the 2002 Commonwealth Games, the complex has the greatest concentration of sporting venues in Europe. Its centrepiece is the **City of Manchester Stadium**, which is now the home of Manchester City Football Club. There are guided tours of the stadium and there is a great museum dedicated to the good and bad times of the 'Blues'.

Sportcity also includes the Manchester Regional Arena, the National Squash Centre, the Tennis Centre, the English Institute of Sport and the **Manchester Velodrome**, where many of Britain's Olympic cycling medallists trained.

At the entrance to Sportcity, there is a huge metal sculpture, which looks like an exploding firework and is known as the **B of the Bang**. It was inspired by a quotation from sprinter Linford Christie, who said that he started his races, not merely on the 'bang' of the starting pistol, but on the B of the bang!

As the sculpture has exploded in an unintentional way since its erection, with some of the metal spikes crashing to the ground, the structure may have to be dismantled temporarily.

Glass roof dedicated to Sir William Walton, Oldham

Above: Walking by the Canal, Diggle   Below right: Newbank Garden Centre, Dobcross

Above: Pieces of Paradise, Uppermill   *Above: B of the Bang at Sport City*

Places to Visit Greater Manchester

Ashton-under-Lyne Market

Outdoor market: every day except
Tuesday and Sunday
Tuesday: flea market
Sun: table top market
Last Sunday each month: farmers'
market

Bolton Museum & Art Gallery

Le Mans Crescent, Bolton
☎ 01204 332211
Open: Mon to Sat 9am–5pm
Closed: Sun and Bank Holidays

Bury Market

Bury
Outdoor Market: Wed, Fri, Sat
Indoor market: every day

Chill Factor Indoor Ski Centre

Trafford Way
☎ 0161 749 2222
Lessons: 8am–10pm daily
Recreational: Mon, Tue 9.30am–11pm
Wed 7.30am–11pm, Thu to Sun
9.30am–11pm

City of Manchester Stadium and Tour

Sportcity, Manchester
☎ 0161 438 7824
Open: Mon to Sat 9.30am–4.30pm
Sun and Bank Holidays 11am–3pm

Ellenroad Mill

Milnrow
☎ 07789 802632
Steam days: first Sunday of each month
11am–4pm

Gallery Oldham

Union Street, Oldham
☎ 0161 770 4653
Open: Mon to Sat 10am–5pm

Great House Barn

Rivington
☎ 01204 697738
Open: every day except Christmas Day

Haigh Hall Country Park

Wigan
For details of events etc., contact 01942
832895

Hall i' th' Wood

Green Way, Bolton
☎ 01204 332370
Open: Nov to Easter: Sat, Sun only
12pm–5pm. Easter to Nov: Wed to Sun
12pm–5pm

Imperial War Museum North

The Quays, Trafford
☎ 0161 836 4000
Open 7 days a week:
1 Mar to 2 Nov: 11am–6pm
3 Nov to 28 Feb: 10am–5pm
Closed 24–26 Dec

Millyard Gallery

Uppermill
☎ 01457 870410
Open: daily 10am–5pm; Sun 11am–
4pm; closed Tue

Old Trafford/Manchester United Tour

Trafford
☎ 0161 868 8000
Open: Mon–Sun 9.30am–5pm

Saddleworth Crafts Cooperative and John McCombs' Gallery

Delph
☎ 01457 874 705
Open: 9.30am–5pm, every day except Mon

Saddleworth Museum

Uppermill
☎ 01457 874093
Open: Easter to Oct: Mon to Sat 10am–4.30pm; Sun 12pm–4pm
Winter: Mon–Sun 1pm–4pm

Smithills Hall

Smithills Dean Road, Bolton
☎ 01204 332377
Open: Easter to 1 Nov: Tue–Fri and Sun 12pm–5pm
1 Nov to Easter: Fri and Sun: 12pm–5pm

The Lowry

(includes art galleries, theatres, restaurants)
Salford Quays
☎ 0870 787 5780
Galleries open: Sun–Fri 11am–5pm, Sat 10am–5pm

Trafford Centre

Trafford
Open: Mon to Fri 10am–10pm
Sat 9am–9pm, Sun: 12pm–6pm
Cinemas and restaurants open until later

Trencherfield Steam Engine

Wigan Pier
☎ 01942 828020
Open: Mon, Tue, Thu, Fri 10am–4pm
Wed: closed
Sat 10am–1pm

TOURIST INFORMATION CENTRES

Ashton-under-Lyne

Wellington Road, behind Town Hall
☎ 0161 343 4343

Bolton

Le Mans Crescent
☎ 01204 334321

Bury

Market Street
☎ 0161 253 5111

Oldham

Tommyfield Market
☎ 0161 627 1024

Saddleworth

Saddleworth Museum
☎ 01457 870 336

Salford

The Lowry
☎ 0161 848 8601

Wigan

Trencherfield Mill
☎ 01942 825 677

3. Lancaster & Morecambe Bay

Lancaster

Lancaster is Edinburgh in miniature. Like the Scottish capital, the city is overlooked by a huge castle and its streets are lined with grey stone buildings, whose sturdiness is matched by their architectural quality. As in Edinburgh, the greyness should not be mistaken for drabness, not only because it helps to create a wonderful old-town atmosphere, but also because it is offset by the colourful character of a vibrant cultural, commercial and tourist centre.

Ashton Memorial in Williamson Park Lancaster

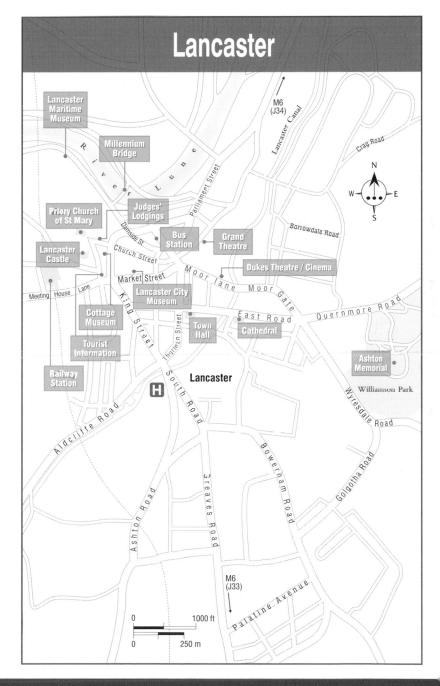

Lancaster

From Romans to Royals

Lancaster began life as Loncastre, which translates as a fort on the Lune. Built by the Romans, the garrison occupied a strategically important promontory on the river's south bank. After the Romans left, their military stronghold evolved into a town, which became the capital of the newly formed county of Lancashire in 1182.

Although Lancashire's administrative offices are now based in Preston, Lancaster is still classed as the county town. It also has long-standing royal connections, because the House of Lancaster is a branch of the Royal Family and the Duchy of Lancaster holds large estates for the Queen, who even carries the title 'Duke of Lancaster'.

Motorists travelling north on the M6 motorway catch their first glimpse of Lancaster when the bright buildings of **Lancaster University** come into view. Founded in the 1960s as one of seven new universities, the campus was developed on a site at Bailrigg, three and a half miles (5.5km) south of the city. Architects Peter Shepherd and Charles Epstein designed the university buildings to look like a Mediterranean hilltop village when viewed from afar. Judge for yourself!

The first sighting of the city from the motorway is even more spectacular. A short distance beyond the university buildings, a huge edifice looms up out of thick woodland on the left flank of the road. Built in gleaming-white Portland stone, topped by a green dome

and fashioned in a flamboyant baroque style, the building looks like St Paul's Cathedral transported to the summit of a Lancashire hill.

This giant Edwardian folly is the **Ashton Memorial,** commissioned in 1906 as a memorial to his late wife by Lord Ashton, a millionaire manufacturer of oilcloth and linoleum. Before exploring the city, it is worth making a short diversion to the memorial by following the brown tourist signs. After standing in awe below the massive structure, visitors can enjoy the memorial's changing art exhibitions and ascend to the gallery, where there is a fabulous panoramic view that embraces Morecambe Bay, the Lakeland Fells, Blackpool Tower and the Isle of Man.

The memorial is surrounded by **Williamson Park**, which was laid out in a former quarry by Lord Ashton's father, James Williamson. In more recent years, it has been extended to a total of 54 acres (22 hectares). As well as woodland walks, punctuated by sudden and unexpected views of the memorial, the park contains a butterfly house, a 'Mini-Beast Cave', which is full of creepy-crawlies, an animal garden, an enclosure for free-flying foreign birds and the **Lancaster Sundial**, where visitors can tell the time by casting their own shadow on bronze panels.

Williamson Park is a short distance from central Lancaster, where motorists become caught up in a gyratory system that makes a clockwise circumnavigation of the city centre. Much as on the *Périphérique* in Paris, drivers are likely to find themselves looping the loop for a second time unless they keep a careful eye on signs for slip roads leading to local attractions.

The logical starting point for an exploration is **Lancaster Castle**, which dominates the city from the summit of a high crag. With its battlemented, dark-stone facade and massive gatehouse, it has a forbidding presence in keeping with its grim past and its continuing use as a court and a prison. Parts of the building are open to the public, who have an opportunity to see grisly exhibits such as branding irons and treadmills, as well as the underground dungeons where the Lancashire Witches were kept before their trial in 1612 (for details, see the chapter covering Pendle).

Visitors can inspect a record of 200 executions, only 43 of which were for convicted murderers. A database of hundreds of transportations, mostly ordered as punishment for petty crimes, is of particular interest to Australian visitors researching their family history. The guided tour of the castle includes a visit to the remarkable ten-sided Shire Hall, which was added to the castle in the eighteenth century.

The **Priory Church of St Mary** shares the hilltop site with the castle and is an equally dominant presence on the skyline. It is not surprising to find that there are superb 360-degree views from the top of its tower, which is a very tall, well-proportioned structure in the darkest of dark stone. Visitors to this impressive church should look out for a square-topped Saxon doorway, fabulous choir stalls with tall, decorated oak canopies and three elaborate brass candelabras donated by William Heysham in 1717.

Castle Hill, immediately below the castle and the priory church, has some very interesting buildings. These include the **Judges' Lodgings**, a seventeenth-century town house, where there is a display of furniture, porcelain, silverware and paintings, as well as a recreation of an Edwardian schoolroom. The nearby **Cottage Museum** is a tiny eighteenth-century dwelling, where visitors are greeted by a 'Victorian housekeeper'.

Half-buried in the hillside below the castle, there is Merchants, an atmospheric cellar bar and restaurant. In the lower town, there are lots of Italian restaurants and plenty of pubs serving good food, including one with the wonderful name of Fibber McGee's. What's more, café bars and coffee shops are springing up everywhere – Starbucks and Caffè Nero even occupy adjacent premises.

The shopping centre in the lower town includes covered shopping precincts in St Nicholas Arcades and Marketgate, and a wide range of stores. Book lovers will be pleased to know that there are two branches of Waterstone's and anyone with a sweet tooth will want to look out for Humbugs, a fabulous sweet emporium with a huge selection of the type of sweet treats that older readers will remember from their childhood.

The Market Square, which hosts outdoor market stalls from Monday to Saturday, is overlooked by a large Georgian building that is an elegant home for the **Lancaster City Museum**, where there is an impressive collection of paintings, as well as exhibits designed to trace the history of the city and the pedigree of the King's Own Royal Regiment. A tapas bar called 1725, which stands on the perimeter of the Market Square, has a plaque which reads: 'Bonnie Prince Charlie was proclaimed Regent by the Jacobite Army near here on 24th November, 1745.'

Before leaving this fascinating city, it is worth wandering down to St

George's Quay, where many of the tall buildings date from the days when Lancaster was a major port. Some of these structures have been sensitively converted into apartments and, where there were gaps in the streetscape, new residential blocks have been added in a style that cleverly echoes that of the original quayside buildings.

A former Custom House on the quayside accommodates the **Lancaster Maritime Museum**, which is marketed to visitors as a reminder of the city's maritime glory days. It could be argued that 'glory days' is something of an unfortunate term, because the city's wealth in the Georgian era rested in large part on its involvement in the slave trade!

Gateway, Lancaster Castle

Opposite page: Museum and Market Square, Lancaster

Morecambe Bay

With the resort of Morecambe just four miles (6.5km) away, Lancaster is the gateway to Morecambe Bay, a magnificent sweep of coast that stretches in a great arc from Glasson Dock to the edge of the Lake District.

The bay has achieved notoriety because of a tragic accident on the night of 5 February 2005, when 23 Chinese cockle-pickers were drowned by the incoming tide, which is said to rush in 'as fast as a horse can run'.

However, Morecambe Bay has much more positive claims to fame. In fact, it was named as one as the 'Seven Natural Wonders of the North' on a BBC television programme in 2005. The sunsets visible from its shores are often magnificent and, on a clear day, the views of the Lakeland Fells are mesmerising.

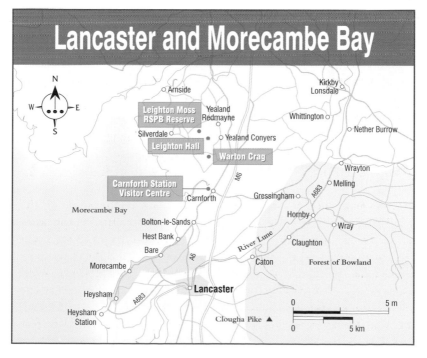

Lancaster and Morecambe Bay

The artist Turner was so impressed on his first visit in 1797 that he made a return trip to make preliminary sketches for a series of evocative paintings of distant views of the Cumberland Fells.

The bay is recognised throughout the world as an important bird habitat, because it is a wintering site for more than 200,000 wildfowl and wading birds. Thousands of humans are also drawn to the area each year by the opportunity to take part in the famous Cross Bay Walk, a guided journey across the Kent estuary from Arnside to Kents Bank, near Grange-over-Sands.

Heysham

Although Morecambe and its bay can be reached from Lancaster in less than ten minutes by following the A589, it is worth taking a diversion along the A683 through **Heysham** (pronounced 'Hee-sham', rather than 'Hay-sham').

The distant view of Heysham is dominated by two ugly box-like structures of gargantuan proportions, which turn out to be the reactor housings of twin nuclear power stations. However, visitors should not be frightened off, because the nearby village is very worthy of a visit, not only for its visual merits as a very attractive coastal settlement, but also for its three remarkable clifftop features.

On the very edge of the cliff, there are six parallel hollow graves hewn out of a piece of solid rock. The origin of the remarkable **Rock Graves of Heysham** is unclear. Why are they in this exposed location? Why are they too small for adults of normal build? Why would anyone go to the trouble of making

tombs by hacking into solid rock? Why have the graves been placed side by side? Whatever the answers to these tantalising questions, the graves make an unforgettable sight and the views across the bay from here are no less memorable.

Close by the graves, there are the ruins of **St Patrick's Chapel**, which amount to little more than a south wall with a round-arched doorway, a gabled end-wall at right angles to it and a few foundations. According to legend, the chapel was built by St Patrick to mark his first landing in England when he arrived from Ireland on a conversion mission. However, this version of events dates the building as fifth century, whereas archaeological evidence suggests that it is rather later – although still pre-Norman. Once again, the visitor is faced with tantalising questions about the true origin of the building. The seaward view obtained by looking through the one remaining window of the chapel is magnificent!

In a hollow below the chapel, there stands **St Peter's Church**, a neat little building of Norman origin. Noting that some of the pews are sited by the windows that look out over the bay, local writer Elizabeth Ashworth has said, 'You could probably draw more divine inspiration from that view than from a dozen long sermons.'

The village that nestles between the cliff and the sea is one of the most attractive in Lancashire. It has several seventeenth-century cottages, most of which have mullions, stone lintels and date stones. Thanks to the efforts of proud locals, Heysham has twice been given a Gold Small Village Award in the Britain in Bloom contest.

It pays to tread with care on the lower slopes of the village street because the sea comes right up to its foot and laps over the paving. A sign warns of the danger of quicksand. To the south of the village, away from the quicksands, there is a port with ferry services to the Isle of Man and Belfast. Our next destination is Morecambe, which lies three miles (5km) to the north of Heysham.

Shrimps, Nettles and Hidgy Pidgy

Lancashire is famed for its speciality foods and Morecambe Bay is no exception. Locally-caught brown shrimps are Morecambe's best-known delicacy. Boiled in butter and spices until tender and then sealed with butter, they are renowned for their tender taste and unique texture.

Heysham is known for nettle beer and nettle tea, both of which are said to have tonic properties. As well as dispensing nettle tea at Bell's Cottage Tea Rooms in Heysham, Cherie Bell produces nettle tea bags, many of which are exported to China of all places!

In addition to nettles, the ingredients that go into nettle tea include root ginger and lemon peel. Readers will be reassured to learn that the nettles are grown in compliance with the Soil Association's organic standards. Cherie Bell also produces Hidgy Pidgy Scones, containing butter and, of course, nettles.

Morecambe

Let's be honest, **Morecambe** has seen better days. The resort was first established in the late nineteenth century and became very popular in the mid-twentieth century, when it was a favourite destination for holidaymakers from many parts of Scotland and Northern England. The town also had a very high profile nationally because it hosted the Miss Great Britain Contest for over 30 consecutive years.

Then, with the advent of low-cost flights to places with guaranteed sun, Morecambe went into a sad decline. The indoor waterworld closed, the pleasure beach ceased to function and the two piers disappeared.

Now for the good news: an imaginative regeneration scheme, launched in 1995 and known as the **Tern Project**, is gradually bringing about a revival in the town's fortunes. Generous grants have been obtained to build new sea defences; the five-mile (8km) long promenade has been remodelled and public works of art celebrating Morecambe Bay's bird life have been positioned at intervals along its length; and the renovated **Stone Jetty**, which is located immediately behind the Midland Hotel, has been inlaid with a maze, a magpie hopscotch, tongue-twisters and word searches – great fun for children (and adults!). A café at the end of the jetty offers welcome relaxation after all the fun.

Although all these features are very attractive and eye-catching, one new feature above all others has caught the imagination of visitors. This is Graham Ibbeson's **Statue of Eric Morecambe**, which was unveiled by the Queen in 1999. It stands at the heart of the promenade and depicts the famous comedian in the dancing pose that so many remember from his *Morecambe and Wise* television shows – Eric skipping along with one arm held aloft. Visitors queue to mimic the pose and have their photographs taken alongside the statue, while others can be heard happily singing a rendition of 'Bring Me Sunshine'. Although settled weather cannot be guaranteed at Morecambe, this statue seems to have brought perpetual sunshine to the resort.

Bring Me Sunshine

'Bring Me Sunshine' was the signature tune of Morecambe and Wise, a comedy duo who dispensed sunshine to millions of television viewers. Christened John Eric Bartholomew, Eric was born in Morecambe in 1926. His mother paid for him to attend dancing classes, which he hated at the time. However, in later life, his dancing skills stood him in good stead. As a youngster, Eric won lots of talent contests, one of which gave him an audition with Jack Hylton, where he met another young talent by the name of Ernest Wiseman.

A couple of years later, the pair met up again and decided to form a double act. Successful appearances on Sunday Night at the London Palladium as Morecambe and Wise (which had a rather better ring to it than Bartholomew and Wiseman) brought them further television work, culminating in the Morecambe and Wise Show, which ran from 1968 until 1984. Three months after their final Christmas show, Eric died of a heart attack at the age of 58.

He had suffered his first heart attack in 1968 while driving to a hotel in Leeds. The man who found him slumped in his car and drove him to hospital had only ever driven a tank before. Just before leaving the comedian in intensive care, Eric's rescuer asked for his autograph, saying, 'Before you go, can you sign this piece of paper?' Eric thought that it would be the last autograph he would ever sign!

Above left: Staircase, Midland Hotel, Morecambe Above right: Rock tombs, Heysham

St Patrick's Chapel, Heysham

Tom Bloxham of the developers Urban Splash has shown his confidence in Morecambe's future by splashing out on a complete renovation and reopening of the **Midland Hotel**, one of the most celebrated Art Deco buildings in the country – white walled, subtly curved and bearing more than a passing resemblance to a great passenger liner at sea. In its heyday, the hotel was visited by the likes of Wallis Simpson, Laurence Olivier and Coco Chanel, who is said to have landed her seaplane on the beach.

Optimists have billed the renovation of this great building as Morecambe's great 'White Hope', while pessimists have inevitably predicted that it will be a 'White Elephant'. Judged on my observation of the number of people enjoying the fantastic sea views and fine food in the coffee bars and restaurants of the hotel, the hope expressed by the optimists is well founded. Don't fail to look up to the decorated ceiling of the great Art Deco spiral staircase and do make sure that you sit in the green chairs that have the largest backrests and the biggest arms that you've ever seen!

Attention is now focused on another of Morecambe's architectural treasures. Since its closure in 1977, the **Winter Gardens Theatre** has deteriorated alarmingly. However, a long campaign for its restoration has led to its purchase by a preservation trust, whose trustees are hopeful that the building can be saved.

Some of Morecambe's fabric may have decayed in recent years, but it has always possessed three wonderful natural assets: miles of golden sand, spectacular views and a huge variety of bird life. As the binoculars suspended from the neck of his statue indicate, Eric Morecambe was one of the many keen birdwatchers who regard Morecambe Bay as a place of pilgrimage.

Happy Mount Park, at Bare, on the northern edge of Morecambe, has always been a place of pilgrimage for families visiting the resort. Its attractions include a splash park, swing boats, a miniature railway, an indoor play area and a café. Much more than the bare necessities in a public park, you might say!

Carnforth

Whereas Morecambe is known for its links with a much-loved comedian, our next port of call is famed for its connection with a classic movie. **Carnforth**, which is reached by taking the A5105 from Morecambe, was used as a location for David Lean's 1946 film *Brief Encounter*, which starred Trevor Howard as Alec and Celia Johnson as Laura.

The refreshment room at the station has been faithfully restored to resemble the set that was used to represent the place where Laura and Alec first met; the platform clock that played such a significant part in the film is still there and the station buildings have been converted into the **Carnforth Station Visitor Centre**.

As well as watching a video of *Brief Encounter* and inspecting many other exhibits related to the movie and its actors, visitors can trace the history of the station from its opening in 1846. Reminders of the days when thousands of servicemen passed through the station on their way to overseas service are particularly poignant. The visitor centre is too good to miss on any visit to this area. What's more, admission is free.

Among the specialist shops in Carnforth's main street, there is one very special attraction – the **Carnforth Book Shop**, which has over 100,000 second-hand and antiquarian books in 14 rooms on the second and third floors. A bibliophile's paradise!

Warton

While Carnforth trades on its associations with *Brief Encounter*, the nearby village of **Warton** celebrates its associations with George Washington, the first president of the United States.

The first members of the Washington family to settle in Warton were seven generations previous to George Washington. Thomas Washington arrived in the hamlet in about 1300 and his great-grandson, Robert Washington, helped to build the tower of **St Oswald's Church**.

Thomas's tower has a handsome profile, but its detailing is masked by the roughcast rendering that has been added to protect it from the effects of the winds that blow across Morecambe Bay. The interior of the church has some impressive stained-glass windows, including an east window patterned by lots of circular hollows that look like bottle bottoms and a deeply coloured window near the font that is the work of Burrows, a local craftsman who also worked at Salisbury Cathedral. It is surprising to find that Burrows was a self-confessed atheist!

Of course, it is not the stained-glass windows that draw visitors to St Oswald's, but the Washington connections. Inside the church, there is a painting of George Washington, which is displayed alongside the coat of arms of the Washington family. This comprises three stars and two stripes and is said to have inspired the design of the Stars and Stripes. It is easy to make comparisons between the coat of arms and the actual design, because the American flag hangs in the nave alongside the Union Jack, except on American Independence Day, when it is flown outside the church.

Other Washington connections include Revd Thomas Washington, who served as vicar of St Oswald's until 1823 and was the last remaining member of the English branch of the Washington family, and Elizabeth Washington, whose gravestone stands just outside the east end of the church. Although the stone is clearly dated 1715, the surface is so badly worn that the rest of the inscription is almost indecipherable – surely it merits a clean-up!

As well as illustrating George Washington's descent from Robert and Elizabeth Washington, the family trees on show in the church indicate that Sir Winston Churchill and Princess Diana were descendants of Robert Kitson of Warton Hall.

After carrying out investigations at the church, many visitors will welcome a relaxing drink at the local pub. As one would expect, it is called the George Washington and carries a portrait of the great man on its inn sign.

Above: Warton

Carnforth Station setting for Brief Encounter

Right: Carnforth Bookshop
Below: Arnside

Below: Silverdale

Warton Crag

Warton is overlooked by **Warton Crag**, a prominent limestone hill that provides extensive views over Morecambe Bay, the Kent estuary, the Lakeland fells and the Yorkshire Dales. The hill itself is a combination of crags, limestone pavements and deciduous woodlands.

Much of the land on and around the crag is protected as a nature reserve, because it has some rare plants and a fine display of rock lichens, as well as being home to an outstanding collection of butterflies. Thanks to three different types of vetches, much of the ground is transformed into a carpet of yellow in May and June. In the height of summer, there is a colourful combination of the yellow flowers of rock rose and purple mats of thyme.

One visitor car park is reached by travelling 100 yards (100m) along Crag Road from its junction with Warton's main street at the Black Bull Inn. There is a further car park 600 yards (600m) to the west.

Leighton Moss

The area immediately north of Warton Crag is **Leighton Moss**, one of the RSPB's most popular nature reserves. As well being a habitat for rare birds, such as bitterns, bearded tits and marsh harriers, the area is home to roe and red deer. In the autumn, thousands of wading birds and ducks descend on the sandflats and saltmarshes. Binoculars are available for hire and there are five birdwatching hides that overlook the shallow meres. The visitor centre and tearoom is located at Myer's Farm, near Silverdale Station.

Silverdale

The coastal village of **Silverdale** is reached from Warton by taking the road that runs along the western flank of Warton Crag and Leighton Moss. On arriving at Silverdale, the road makes a winding descent to the shore past pretty cottages. The views are absolutely stunning at any time of day, but especially at sunset.

The village is part of the Arnside and Silverdale Area of Outstanding Natural Beauty, famed as the home of the Lady's Slipper Orchid, which attracts thousands of visitors every year. A nearby headland known as Jack Scout leads to **Jenny Brown's Point**, which provides a view across the bay to Humphrey Head, where, according to legend, the last wolf in England was killed. At Waterslack Farm, there is a shop, café and garden centre.

Arnside

The former fishing village of **Arnside** is located to the north of Silverdale and stands on the estuary where the River Kent enters Morecambe Bay. White-washed houses flank the promenade, from where there is a fine view of the estuary, which is crossed by a very long railway viaduct. The building of the viaduct caused the estuary to silt up and brought about Arnside's demise as a port. It is now a pleasant little holiday resort and the starting point for a world-famous walk across the sands to West Cumbria.

The Sand Pilot

Ever since 1963, Cedric Robinson has been a Queen's Guide to the sands of Morecambe Bay. Between May and September, he leads about 30 walks across the sands from Arnside to Kents Bank, a distance of eight miles (13km). People come from many parts of the world to take part. Conversely, Cedric loves his job so much that he has never been abroad.

With the help of a stick and a whistle, Cedric shepherds his parties across the safe stretches of the sand, which are forever changing. The trickiest part of the walk involves wading across the River Kent by linking hands and forming a human chain. Although in his seventies, Cedric is even prepared to give people piggybacks if they begin to tire, as he did with the famous historian A.J.P. Taylor!

There are some ancient pele towers in the vicinity and the village is overlooked by Arnside Knott, yet another vantage point in an area that has an abundance of wonderful panoramic views.

Leighton Hall

On its journey from Arnside, the road leading to the villages of Yealand Conyers and Yealand Redmayne passes the estate of **Leighton Hall**. Built in grey limestone, this Gothic fantasy is superbly sited in a bowl of woods and parkland below a backdrop of Lake District hills – a better setting for a country house would be hard to find! As well as enjoying guided tours of the hall, visitors can take woodland walks and wander into the nineteenth-century walled garden, with its fragrant herb patch and ornamental vegetable plot.

Although the hall dates back to 1246, its fabulous Gothic frontage was commissioned in 1822 by Richard Gillow, the grandson of Robert Gillow, who was the founder of a famous Lancaster firm of furniture-makers. When Richard retired from the family business, he lived the life of a country squire at Leighton Hall and his descendants still live in the house.

Yealand Conyers and Yealand Redmayne

The small, attractive villages of **Yealand Conyers** and **Yealand Redmayne** are situated to the east of Leighton Hall. Quaker leader George Fox (see the chapter on Pendle) preached in both villages in 1652 and the Quaker meeting house in Yealand Conyers is still in regular use. The village pub, the New Inn, dates from 1680.

It is now a straightforward journey back to Lancaster via the A6 or the M6.

Places to Visit
Lancaster & Morecambe Bay

LANCASTER

Ashton Memorial
Williamson Park ☎ 01524 33318
Open daily: 10am–5pm

Cottage Museum
Castle Hill ☎ 01524 64637
Open: Easter to Sep 2pm–5pm

Judges' Lodgings
Church Street ☎ 01524 32808
Open: Easter to 30 June and Oct 1pm–
4pm Mon to Fri, 12pm–4pm Sat, Sun
Jul, Aug, Sep: 10am–4pm Mon to Fri;
12pm–4pm Sat, Sun

Lancaster Castle
Castle Parade ☎ 01524 64998
Guided tours: 10.30am–4pm

Lancaster City Museum
Market Square ☎ 01524 64637
Daily: 10am–5pm; closed Sun

Lancaster Maritime Museum
St George's Quay ☎ 01524 382264
Open: Easter to Oct 11am–5pm daily,
Nov to Easter 12.30pm–5pm

MORECAMBE BAY

Carnforth Station Visitor Centre
☎ 01524 735165
Open daily, except Monday

Cross Bay Walk, Arnside
Book by ringing 0787 5845693

Leighton Hall
Near Warton ☎ 01524 734474
Open: 1 May to 30 Sep 2pm–5pm Tues
to Fri and Bank Holidays

Leighton Moss Visitor Centre
Myers Farm, Silverdale ☎ 01524 701601
Trails close at dusk

PLACES TO STAY

LANCASTER

Holiday Inn
Near M6 motorway on Caton Road
☎ 0871 423 4931

Lancaster House Hotel
4-star country house hotel just outside
the city ☎ 08458 509508

Royal King's Arms
3-star hotel in city centre, Market Street
☎ 01524 32451

Sun Hotel
4-star hotel in city centre, Church St
☎ 01524 66006

MORECAMBE BAY

Midland Hotel
Boutique-style rooms in superb Art Deco
setting
Marine Road West, Morecambe
☎ 01524 424000

Tourist Information Centres

Lancaster
29 Castle Hill, LA1 1YN ☎ 01524 32878

Morecambe Bay
Old Station Buildings,
Marine Road Central, LA4 4DB
☎ 01524 582808

4. Exploring the Lune Valley from Lancaster

Writing in his *Guide to the Lakes*, Wordsworth recommended that his readers should visit the Lune Valley on their way to Lakeland. The poet Thomas Gray described the view from the banks of the Lune as having 'every feature which constitutes a perfect landscape' and J.M.W. Turner made painting trips to the valley.

With recommendations from these connoisseurs of landscape, this is obviously a place that should not be missed. In fact, the 20-mile (30km) stretch of countryside between Lancaster and Kirkby Lonsdale is one of the finest unspoilt stretches of green and pleasant England. Its attractions include a meandering river crossed by ancient hump-backed bridges; old-world villages with traditional festivals; several historic churches; and one very spectacular castle. There are riverside walking trails and dedicated cycle tracks, with plenty of picnic areas, country pubs and inviting tea rooms along the way.

The Lune Valley

Glasson

Before travelling east from Lancaster along the classic stretch of the Lune Valley, some visitors might wish to make a diversion to the old port of **Glasson**, five miles (8km) south-west of the county town. It is located on the banks of the estuary where the River Lune enters the Irish Sea.

As is the case with many other ports, Glasson is not a pretty place, but it is certainly worth visiting during the Easter Weekend, when it hosts an annual **Maritime Festival**, which includes the biggest gathering in the world of performers of sea songs and shanties. In the specially-erected marquees, there are Punch and Judy shows, dramatic productions and demonstrations of all things nautical, including knot-tying and putting a ship in a bottle. On my last visit to the festival, three stone statues depicting two fishermen and a fishwife turned out to be real people!

The **Port of Lancaster Smoke-house** sells a huge range of smoked

products, from salmon and sea trout to duck and pheasant. Its smoked cheeses include local favourites such as Mrs Kirkham's Lancashire and Grandma Singleton's Mature Cheddar.

Attendance at a festival would not be complete without a few pints of beer and a pub meal. The Dalton Arms is a lively local that occupies three former cottages; the Mill Inn stands by the Lancaster Canal and has been converted from an old grain mill into a 15-bedroom hotel and the Stork is a very attractive former coaching inn situated at Condor Green, on the road between Glasson and Lancaster.

Crook O'Lune

The A683 Lancaster to Kirkby Lonsdale road runs close to the south bank of the River Lune all along its length and provides easy access to the valley's attractions. One of the most celebrated beauty spots is **Crook O'Lune**, which is located five miles (8km) east of Lancaster, from which it can also be reached by the cycle track or the footpaths that run through the River Lune Millennium Park – bicycles are available for hire at Lancaster Station (01524 389410).

Crook O'Lune takes its name from a large arc made by the river at this point, where it also runs under an old toll bridge and a former railway bridge (now a footpath and cycleway). As well as being provided with a car park, a picnic area, toilets and a café, visitors are treated to a magnificent view of the valley and a distant prospect of Ingleborough, the second highest peak in the Yorkshire Dales (Whernside is the highest).

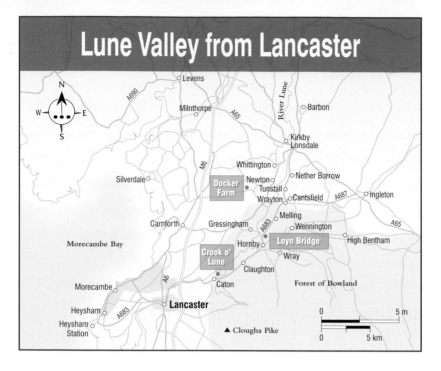

Lune Valley from Lancaster

Claughton

After leaving Crook O'Lune, the A683 passes through **Claughton**, the location of the Fenwick Arms, a gastropub with an open log fire and home-cooked food sourced locally.

Wray

Before reaching Hornby, the next village along the A683, it is worth taking the B6480 to **Wray**, a village nestling in the foothills of the Forest of Bowland. The streets are lined with attractive stone-built cottages, some of considerable antiquity, and there are two inviting pubs: the New Inn and the George and Dragon.

Wray is famed for its annual Scarecrow Festival, which takes place in the week leading up to May Day, when home-made scarecrows appear all over the village. On the Bank Holiday itself, there is a fair, a road-race and a parade of giant scarecrows. The villagers even stage an annual maggot race!

It is worth travelling a few yards beyond the village to **Bridge House Farm and Tearooms**, not only because the locally-sourced food is delicious, but also because the surroundings, both within and without, are superb. The tea room is sited in an old building that has been sensitively renovated and given a state-of-the-art interior, complete with solid oak floors and a real wood-burning stove. In the grounds, there is a picnic area in a great spot by the river, as well as a children's play area.

The farm marks the start of the footpath through the **Roeburndale Valley**, a wooded area where the birds include lapwing, curlew, green woodpecker and common redstart, and the plants include wood sorrel and marsh marigold.

Hornby

Rather than returning to the main road and turning right for **Hornby**, it is possible to reach the village by taking a minor road from Wray. Both routes offer stunning views of **Hornby Castle**, which stands on the summit of a hill and dominates the village as though it were the castle of a feudal manor. The castle was actually founded in feudal times, but the keep dates from the fifteenth century and the rest of the house was remodelled in a romantic style in the eighteenth and nineteenth centuries.

Unfortunately, this striking edifice is normally closed to the public, because it is a private family home. However, the grounds do open on Snowdrop Sunday in February and for the Shades of Autumn weekend in October. The castle is occasionally used for special events, such as old vehicle rallies, and, not surprisingly, it is in demand as a location for films.

Although the village of Hornby suffers from heavy through traffic, it has some very nice houses and a church with a tower that is unusual, not only because it is octagonal but also because it has an upper section that is askew from the lower part. A notable shop in the town is the Spirit of Andes, which specialises in knitwear made from the wool of the alpaca, a small llama-like animal from South America.

Loyn Bridge

Just beyond Hornby, there is a left turn to **Loyn Bridge**, a very impressive three-arched span, which dates from 1684. Next to the bridge, there is the mound of **Castle Stede**, a motte and bailey castle that guarded the river crossing in Norman times. The views of the bridge from the banks of the Lune are superb.

Families visiting the area might like to continue their diversion from the main road by carrying on to **Arkholme** and **Docker Park Farm**, a working farm where visitors can meet the animals, feed the lambs, take tractor rides and collect eggs. The visitor centre has a shop and tea room.

Melling and Tunstall

The next two villages along the route, **Melling** and **Tunstall**, are notable for their churches. St Wilfred's at Melling is an impressive building of thirteenth-century origin, which is sometimes known as the Cathedral of the Lune. The Church of St John the Baptist in Tunstall was used as the model for Brocklebridge Church in *Jane Eyre* – Charlotte Bronte and her sisters would often undertake the two-mile (3km) walk from their school at Cowan Bridge to attend Sunday Service in Tunstall.

Nether Burrow

Nether Burrow, situated just a mile up the road from Tunstall, is the location of the Highwayman, where a log fire provides a warm welcome in winter and a walled garden makes for a pleasant outdoor seating area in summer. The menu, which is heavily based on local produce and traditional regional dishes, is inspired by Nigel Haworth, chef patron of Northcote Manor, the wines have been selected by Craig Bancroft, also of Northcote Manor, and the Thwaites' ales include the famous Lancaster Bomber beer, judged as the best ale in England at the European Beer Show in 2007.

Kirkby Lonsdale

The A683 terminates at the A6, just south of **Kirkby Lonsdale** (pronounced 'Kerby'), an ancient market town that stands close to the point where the three counties of Lancashire, Yorkshire and Cumbria meet. At the entrance to the village, there is an ancient Devil's Bridge, which spans the rock-strewn river in dramatic fashion.

Legend has it that the devil promised an old woman that he would build a bridge in exchange for the first soul to cross it. When the bridge was finished, the woman threw a piece of bread over the bridge and her dog chased after it, so thwarting the devil

Devil's Bridge, Kirkby Lonsdale

Thanks to its combination of dignified Georgian buildings, quaint cottages and traditional shop fronts, Kirkby Lonsdale has a delightful appearance. What's more, its attractions extend well beyond its aesthetic appeal, because there are almost sixty shops in the town, plus lots of places to eat and drink.

St Mary's Church is an attractive bit of everything: its origin is Norman, but it is built on an Anglo-Saxon site; many of its fittings are Victorian, but the pulpit is seventeenth-century. Direction signs in the churchyard point to a place where there is a view of the River Lune that drew lavish praise from John Ruskin, who said, 'I do not know in all my own country, still less in France or Italy, a place more naturally divine.' This beauty spot marks a fitting end to our journey along one of England's most attractive valleys.

Places to Visit The Lune Valley

Bridge House Farm and Tea Room

Wray (contains information point on local walks)
☎ 01524 222496
Open: Tues to Sun 10am – 5pm in summer; 10am – 4pm in winter

Cycle Hire

Contact Lancaster Station on
☎ 01524 389410

Docker Park Farm Visitor Centre

Arkholme
☎ 01524 221331
Open: Mid-Feb to Oct: every day 10.30am – 5pm
Nov to mid-Feb weekends only 10.30am – 4pm
Closed Christmas to New Year

5. Preston & the Fylde Coast

Preston

The people of Preston have often referred to their town as 'Proud Preston', but they were almost bursting with pride when the town was awarded city status in 2002 and became England's fiftieth city in the fiftieth year of the Queen's reign.

The Harris Art Gallery, Preston

Aside from this new distinction, **Preston** has a number of other claims to fame. It was the first town in England to be lit by gas (1815); it is home to the world's oldest continuous branch of the Mormon church; its main Roman Catholic church, St Walburge's, has the tallest spire in England that is not on a cathedral; its bypass, now part of the M6, was the first stretch of motorway

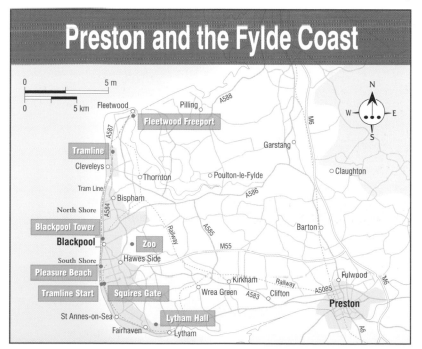

Preston and the Fylde Coast

in Britain; and its football club, Preston North End, was a founder member of the Football League and was the first to be crowned English champions.

Fittingly, Preston is home to the **National Football Museum**, where there is an almost bewildering display of archives, photographs, videos, sound archives and interactive displays celebrating the 'beautiful game'. Visitors can inspect scores of iconic artefacts, including the ball from the 1966 World Cup Final and the shirt that Maradona wore in the infamous 'hand of God' game, or they can take up various interactive challenges, including an invitation from Gary Lineker and Alan Hansen to become television football pundits.

A balcony window provides a spectacular view into Preston North End's Deepdale stadium and a sculpture known as **'The Splash'**, which is located at the entrance to the museum, depicts Tom Finney, the club's legendary winger. The Hall of Fame celebrates many of football's other great players, including women soccer stars, as well as the game's most successful managers. And all this for no admission charge!

A Living Legend

The statue of Sir Tom Finney outside the National Football Museum is modelled on the 1956 Sports Photograph of the Year which shows him beating two Chelsea defenders on a waterlogged Stamford Bridge pitch.

Tom made his England debut just one month after his first appearance for Preston North End in 1946. He went on to gain 76 caps and score 30 goals for his country. As a two-footed player, he was able to play left-wing, right-wing and even centre-forward for England. He had superb balance, could spray pinpoint passes and head and shoot with power – in other words, he was the complete footballer. His ability was best summed up by the great Liverpool manager Bill Shankly, who said: 'Tom Finney would have been great in any team, in any match and in any age, even in an overcoat.'

Because his father insisted that he complete his apprenticeship after he had been signed up by Preston, he was able to earn a second wage as a plumber, but he turned down the chance to make a fortune from football when he rejected a move to Palermo in 1952, which would have given him a £10,000 signing-on fee. Instead, he remained with Preston throughout his career, playing 433 games for the club and scoring 187 goals. He is now the president of the club. The contrast with modern so-called superstars, in terms of ability, loyalty and attitude to financial rewards, is very evident!

Preston is also home to the **Harris Museum and Art Gallery**, which overlooks the city's impressive central square. The building is a grand neoclassical edifice of 1893 and its eclectic painting collection includes works by celebrated British artists such as Walter Sickert, Graham Sutherland, John Piper and Lucian Freud. However, the gallery's most popular painting is Sir James Gunn's *Pauline in the Yellow Dress*, which is a very striking (and colourful) portrait of the artist's second wife and was once described by the *Daily Mail* as 'the Mona Lisa of 1944'. A gallery devoted to ceramics and glass is a recent addition to this fine museum.

Preston has three other museums: the **Ribble Steam Museum**, which offers a three-mile (5km) trip by steam train alongside the River Ribble; the **Museum of the Queen's Lancashire Regiment**, sited at Fulwood Barracks; and the **British Commercial Vehicle Museum**, located at nearby Leyland.

Thanks to the plethora of museums, a good shopping area, which includes a modern precinct, no fewer than seven public parks and some fine Victorian buildings at the city's core, Preston is worthy of a visit, but it is far from being a pretty town, because the demise of the port and the death of the local cotton industry have resulted in a fair amount of deprivation and a good deal of unsightliness. However, regeneration efforts are currently in full swing, most noticeably in the old dockland area, where brand new commercial, residential and leisure premises are already in place.

The road alongside the docks heads for the **Fylde Coast**, famed throughout the land for its golden sands, breezy promenades, Victorian piers, seaside postcards, tyrannical landladies, Blackpool rock, 'Kiss Me Quick' hats, terrifying fairground rides and beach donkeys.

The Fylde Coast

The Fylde Coast is reached from Preston by following the A583, which runs parallel with the north bank of the Ribble estuary. Along the way, there are two places worthy of a stop-off: **Dobbies Garden Centre**, near Clifton, and the village of **Wrea Green**, just south of the main road.

Dobbies is a very large garden centre, partially set in an impressive glass-fronted building. It has a huge range of plants, flowers, gardening equipment, garden furniture and homeware. On the ground floor, there is a very attractive restaurant area known as the Greenapple.

To gain a clear picture of **Wrea Green,** simply conjure up an image of the archetypal English village, with a church and a pub set alongside a duck pond and a village green that also serves as a cricket pitch. In fact, Wrea Green once had no fewer than three ponds – until the local cricket team asked for two of them to be filled in. The green is the largest in Lancashire, and surely the most picturesque.

Refreshment opportunities in and around the village are many and varied. They include the popular Grapes Inn, which stands in a perfect location on the edge of the green, and a Thai restaurant, which is also in the centre of the village. A country house hotel known as the Villa, Rigby's Farmhouse, which serves traditional home-cooked English food, and celebrity chef Nigel Smith's restaurant at Rigby Hall Village are all just a short walk away.

Rather than returning from Wrea Green to the A583 and heading straight for Blackpool, follow the meandering country lanes to genteel **Lytham**, which is the southern half of **Lytham St Annes**.

Lytham

On the way into Lytham, there are two attractions that should not be missed: a grand country house and Booth's supermarket. Yes, you read that correctly – a supermarket that is a tourist attraction!

Lytham Hall is approached along a winding drive, which suddenly opens up to give a surprise view of what is best described as a giant doll's house – a tall, symmetrical, red-bricked building with three storeys and lots of windows, all picked out in white surrounds.

Built between 1752 and 1764, the hall was designed for Thomas Clifton by John Carr of York. It occupies the site of an earlier manor house and a priory that was settled by Benedictine monks from Durham. Henry Talbot de Vere Clifton, the last Clifton to own the hall, gambled away the family fortune at an alarming rate. When he died in 1975, the estate had already passed to his main creditors, the Guardian Royal Exchange insurance company. However, thanks to a very generous donation by British Aerospace, the Friends of Lytham Hall managed to acquire and save this superb building, which is operated by the Heritage Trust for the North West.

Guided tours are available of the interior of the hall, which has elegant Georgian rooms hung with many fine portraits and a superb staircase supported by Corinthian columns and crowned by Giuseppe Cortese's depiction of Jupiter as creator of the universe. In the grounds, there is a mound that once supported a windmill, a sculpture of Diana the Huntress, and an eighteenth-century dovecote with a revolving ladder that enabled egg-collectors to reach the 850 nesting boxes.

Next stop: the supermarket!

Booth's superstore, on Haven Road, is an attractive venue on three counts. Firstly, unlike many supermarkets, it does not have the appearance of an ugly aircraft hangar, but was actually designed by an architect with a feel for material and geometry. The exterior is nicely curved and the interior is uncluttered and has wide aisles. Secondly, Booth's was founded in 1847 by a local boy made good. Nineteen-year-old Edwin Henry Booth borrowed £80 in goods from the Preston grocer who taught him his trade and used the money to set up the China House Tea Shop in Blackpool, which became the first Booth's store. There are now 25 Booth's stores across the North West and the company is managed by the fifth generation of the family, who still try to follow Edwin's maxim, which was 'to sell the best goods available in attractive stores, staffed with first-class assistants and to develop our product range'. Thirdly, the curved balcony of the store contains the Artisan Coffee Shop and a splendid exhibition area called the **Fylde Art Gallery**, chiefly

Above: Lytham Hall   Below and inset: St Annes Pier

dedicated to the work of Liverpool artist Richard Ansdell.

Lytham is a seaside resort with no beach, because marsh grass has taken over the Ribble estuary along this part of the coast. However, the lack of sand is compensated for by a huge green, which occupies the space between the promenade and the town. As well as providing great views across the estuary, this green space is a perfect place for picnics, kite-flying and impromptu games of cricket and football. It is also a magnet for photographers and artists, because the white windmill and the adjacent lifeboat house that stand in its midst make for a perfect composition.

Lytham Windmill contains a tourist information centre and a superb exhibition organised and staffed by members of Lytham Heritage Group. As well as exhibitions devoted to the history of the windmill and the milling process, there are tableaux of life in Victorian times. The adjacent lifeboat house is the oldest in England.

Just one block away from the green, there is a very attractive main street with nice boutique shops and pleasant pavement cafés. At **Lowther Gardens**, there are facilities for tennis, bowls and mini-golf. All in all, Lytham is a very pleasant place indeed.

Fairhaven

The little resort of **Fairhaven** is located immediately north of Lytham. Its most prominent landmark is the **White Church**, which was fashioned in pure white faience and completed in 1912. When the distinguished architectural historian Nikolaus Pevsner came across the building, he was not entirely enamoured. He said, 'It stands out by size, by colour, by style, only alas not by quality.' Lots of other critics have been unkind about its mixture of Byzantine, Baroque and Moorish features, but most holidaymakers look fondly upon the building.

If nothing else, the church is a clear marker on the way to **Fairhaven Lake**, a stretch of water that offers great opportunities for messing about in boats, from canoes to rowing boats. For those who prefer to leave the navigation to others, there is a passenger launch called the *Jubilee*. Windsurfers are even allowed on the lake if they bring their own equipment. Adjacent to the lake, there are bowling greens, putting and crazy golf courses, skateboard rinks and no fewer than seven tennis courts!

Lytham St Annes also has four first-class golf courses: Fairhaven; Lytham Green Drive; St Annes Old Links; and Royal Lytham St Annes, which is a famous venue for the Open Championship.

St Annes-on-Sea

Fairhaven marks the southern boundary of **St Annes**, a Victorian holiday resort that has managed to remodel itself for the twenty-first century without losing any of its dignity. It offers vitality without vulgarity and beauty without brashness.

Along this stretch of the Ribble estuary, marsh grass has given way to miles of unspoilt golden sands. In fact, the beach is so extensive and so flat that it is a venue for sand-yacht races.

The superbly restored Victorian pier

is entered through a delightful mock Tudor gateway and its various amusements are neatly contained in a series of covered pavilions.

Immediately south of the pier, there is a pleasure-land known as the **Island**, which has a café bar in a converted railway carriage, a four-screen cinema, a casino, a swimming pool, fairground rides, a pub and a lake where it is possible to 'walk on water' in floating bubbles – great amusement for both the daring participants and the onlookers, who can watch from the balcony of a café, which also has splendid views over the sea.

This is the very essence of St Annes, a place where young and old can share a good time, without one age group spoiling the fun of the other in any way. The theme is continued on the promenade, which has nicely manicured gardens, where adults can stroll at leisure and children can run along winding paths, through grottoes and behind miniature waterfalls.

The promenade is lined with grand villas, hotels, bars and restaurants and the main street, which has a mixture of chain stores and boutique shops, is decked out with flower tubs and colourful little pavilions with sheltered seating areas.

This unrivalled family resort even has a brand new attraction. In a garden immediately north of the pier, there is a statue of the comedian Les Dawson, who lived in the area after marrying for the second time. Unfortunately, the effigy is hardly recognisable as the great man!

Playing For Laughs

Les Dawson began his career as a club pianist but shot to television fame as a comedian after winning the talent show Opportunity Knocks in 1967. He wrote several books and would have liked to have been known for his literary skills, but was loved and admired as a great comedian, with his specialities being deliberately bad piano-playing, the mouthing of words in the manner of the mill workers, who had to communicate with one another over the noise of the looms, and his double act with Roy Barraclough, who played pretentious Cissie Braithwaite as a foil to Les's vulgar Ada Shufflebotham.

Above all, Les Dawson is remembered for his mother-in-law jokes, such as: 'I can always tell when the mother-in-law's coming to stay: the mice throw themselves on the traps'; and 'I took my mother-in-law to Madame Tussaud's Chamber of Horrors and one of the attendants said, 'Keep her moving; we're stocktaking.'

Although Les was born in Collyhurst, he moved to Lytham St Annes when he married his second wife, Tracy. His wife and their daughter unveiled his statue on 23 October 2008 to mark the fifteenth anniversary of his death.

Squires Gate

The seafront road from St Annes to Blackpool passes the enormous **Pontin's Holiday Park** at **Squires Gate**, an updated *Hi-de-Hi* sort of place with a range of activities ranging from go-karting to abseiling.

Blackpool

Whereas St Annes offers vitality without vulgarity, **Blackpool** unashamedly offers vitality with vulgarity.

The famous **Pleasure Beach**, which stands at the southern gateway to the town, has no fewer than ten 'white-knuckle rides', ranging from the Valhalla water-ride to the Big One, Britain''s tallest roller coaster, which rises to a height of 235ft (72m) and has over a mile of track. As well as river caves, a 'gold mine', a flying machine, carousels, an arena for ice-skating and a children's theme park, there is also a famous 'Ghost Train'. The Pleasure Beach's many bars, cafés and restaurants offer a wide choice of refreshment opportunities for anyone who has managed to survive the rides with their appetite intact.

The Pleasure Beach is followed by the **Golden Mile**, with its amusement arcades, waxworks, bingo halls, fortune-tellers, cafés, chip shops, gift shops and a *Doctor Who* exhibition. At the head of the Golden Mile stands **Blackpool Tower**, a dead ringer for the Eiffel Tower but only half as high. At its base, there is the famous Tower Ballroom, as well as other leisure facilities, entertainment venues and a circus.

Summer tourism is boosted in the autumn by the annual **illuminations**, which are, of course, very dazzling indeed and stretch from one end of the town to the other.

Three piers stretch out to sea; there are clubs and pubs in abundance and several theatres which host variety

shows featuring some of the country's top acts. Despite the migration of many of its traditional customers to the Mediterranean resorts, Blackpool is still Britain's most popular resort and is said to have more hotels and B&Bs than the whole of Portugal!

Fleetwood

A number of English towns that discarded their trams are now bringing them back, but Blackpool was never foolish enough to part with them in the first place. The trams operate a frequent service all the way up the coast to **Fleetwood**.

Much of Fleetwood was designed in the 1830s by Decimus Burton, who was employed by Sir Peter Hesketh-Fleetwood for the specific purpose of creating a new holiday resort. The centrepiece of his new town was the semi-circular North Euston Hotel, planned as suitable overnight accommodation for travellers who had taken the train from Euston before transferring to boats bound for Scotland. Unfortunately, this fine plan was dealt a fatal blow when a direct rail route to Scotland was constructed over Shap.

The town was then re-invented as a cargo port, but its fortunes were dealt a second blow when the Manchester Ship Canal opened and other cargo ports were constructed further down the coast.

Fleetwood's third re-invention was as a deep-sea fishing port, but this industry went into severe decline as a result of the Cod Wars of the 1970s.

With three lives lost, Fleetwood has now undergone a fourth renaissance as a shopping destination. The former dock landing arca has been imaginatively transformed into **Fleetwood Freeport**. Fronted by a marina and designed in a style resembling that of a Dutch fishing village, the centre has 45 outlet shops, as well as places to eat and drink. There is also a programme of live events.

The history of Fleetwood and its numerous incarnations is told in the **Fleetwood Museum**, which is housed in one of Decimus Burton's elegant buildings. Visitors can also get some insight into the life of Fleetwood's deep-sea fishermen by boarding the *Jacinta*, a restored trawler which is moored on the quayside.

After concluding this fascinating journey along the Fylde Coast, it is possible to return to Preston by a pleasant cross-country route along the A585 to Kirkham, where there is a link with the A583 to Preston.

Top left: Wrea Green Above left: Lytham Green Above right: Blackpool Tower

Places to Visit Preston & the Flyde Coast

PRESTON

British Commercial Vehicle Museum

Leyland
☎ 01772 451011
Open: April to September: Sun, Tue, Wed, Thu 10am–5pm. October: Sun, Tue 10am–5pm. Closed Nov to Mar

Harris Museum and Art Gallery

Market Square, Preston
☎ 01772 258248
Open: 10am–5pm Mon to Sat, except Tue 11am–5pm. Closed Sun and Bank Holidays.

Museum of the Queen's Lancashire Regiment

Fulwood Barracks
☎ 01772 716543
Open: Tue to Thu 9.30am–4.30pm and other times by appointment.

National Football Museum

Sir Tom Finney Way, Preston
☎ 01772 908442
Open: Tue to Sat 10am–5pm. Sun 11am–5pm. Closed Mon, except Bank Holidays. Closed at kick-off on match days.

Ribble Steam Museum

☎ 01772 728800
See www.ribblesteam.org.uk for operating times.

FYLDE COAST

Blackpool Pleasure Beach

☎ 0871 222 1234
Open: 10.30am–10pm, but times vary throughout the year

Dobbies Garden Centre

Blackpool Road, Preston
☎ 01772 683844
Open: 9am–6pm Mon. Thu, Fri, Sat; 9.30am–6pm Tue; 10.30am–4.30pm Sun

Fleetwood Freeport

Anchorage Road
☎ 01253 877377
Open: 10am–6pm Mon to Sun: 10am–8pm Thu

Fleetwood Museum and Jacinta

Queen's Terrace
☎ 01253 876621
Open Apr to Oct: 11am–4pm Mon to Sat; 1pm–4pm Sun

Fylde Art Gallery

In Booth's supermarket
Open: 8am–6pm Mon to Sat; 11am–5pm Sun

Lytham Hall

Lytham Hall Park

☎ 01253 736652

Open: Conducted tours every Sunday at 2pm, except on the last Sunday in the month and Bank Holidays, when the hall is open for self-guided tours 1.30pm–4.30pm

Lytham Windmill

Lytham Green

☎ 01253 794879

Open: 10.30am–1pm; 2pm–4.30pm in the season

PLACES TO STAY

PRESTON

A good choice of hotels in the city, including:

Holiday Inn

Ringway

☎ 0871 423 4931

Ibis Hotel

Garstang Road

☎ 01772 861800

Preston Marriott–4-star

Garstang Road

☎ 01772 864097

Swallow Preston–3-star

Preston New Road

☎ 01772 877351

GLASSON

The Mill Inn

Condor Green

A Mitchell Hotel in a converted mill in the Lune estuary

☎ 0800 083 7706

TOURIST INFORMATION CENTRES

Blackpool

Victoria Road West

☎ 01253 853378

Bowland Visitor Centre

Beacon Fell

☎ 01995 640557

Fleetwood

Esplanade

☎ 01253 773953

Kirkby Lonsdale

Main Street

☎ 01524 2 71437

Lytham St Annes

Town Hall

☎ 01253 725610

Preston

Guild Hall

☎ 01772 253731

6. Exploring the Forest of Bowland from Preston

It would be hard to find a better place to escape the hustle and bustle of everyday life than the Forest of Bowland, because it is one of the least touched and most attractive areas of countryside in England.

Even the region's designation as an Area of Outstanding Natural Beauty hardly begins to do it justice, for this is an unspoilt land of round-topped moors, deep valleys, meandering streams, winding lanes, hump-backed bridges, ancient inns, isolated farmsteads and villages of warm-brown stone.

Thanks to its remoteness, the forest is also a place where traditional village customs have survived to the present time and where some of the country's most endangered species of birds can still find a haven. There is even a wild boar park.

As a twenty-first century bonus, the Forest of Bowland has some of the best gourmet restaurants in the country, but visitors in search of these culinary delights are advised to use a 'satnav' to thread their way through the maze of country lanes!

The Forest of Bowland is best approached from Preston by taking the B6243 and following signs to Longridge, on the western fringe of the Area of Outstanding Natural Beauty.

Longridge

Longridge is a sizeable village with a range of shops, a Thursday market, a Somerfield store, no fewer than eleven pubs and several eating places. To find its most celebrated restaurant, keep forking left and take signs to Jeffrey Hill and Longridge Golf Club.

The **Longridge Restaurant** stands on the corner of a minor junction

partway up Higher Road. This famous eating place is where Paul Heathcote first brought *Cuisine de Terroir* to North West England by producing regional dishes from ingredients supplied by local farmers. It was not long before customers began arriving in droves to sample gourmet versions of traditional dishes such as jellied eel terrine, black pudding, bread and butter pudding and jam tarts with gingerbread ice cream. In 1994, Paul got his due reward when Longridge became one of only six two-star Michelin restaurants in the country.

Thanks to the success of the Longridge restaurant, Paul Heathcote's empire has grown to include restaurants throughout the North. As a result, you'll be lucky to see the black-suited figure of Paul (once voted The Best Dressed Man in Liverpool) in the restaurant, but the food remains as good as ever and Longridge is still the flagship of the Heathcote chain.

Jeffrey Hill

After passing Paul Heathcote's restaurant, Higher Road veers off to the left to become Forty Acre Lane, which travels along the perimeter of Longridge Golf Club as it climbs to the summit of **Jeffrey Hill**.

Although its name sounds like that of a person, Jeffrey Hill is actually a high-level vantage point that commands magnificent views across a seemingly never-ending landscape of vast untouched stretches of moorland, punctuated by deep valleys and cosy, half-hidden villages and farms. The

temptation to drop into the forest and explore further is overwhelming.

A left turn at the first T-junction leads to **Thornley Hall**, a large seventeenth-century farmhouse that once belonged to the Earl of Derby and now offers self-catering accommodation. A right turn just before the hall, followed by a left turn at the next T-junction, leads to the village of Chipping.

Chipping

Chipping is one of Lancashire's prettiest and best-kept settlements. In fact, it has won Best-Kept Village titles on a number of occasions.

The Church of St Bartholomew stands above the village street and is approached by a three-sided flight of steps. Its tower dates from the Perpendicular period and its nave-cum-chancel is pierced by a dormer that sheds light onto the rood screen. There is an unusual interior feature in the north aisle, where some of the columns are decorated by fourteenth-century carved heads, which are so squashed together that their features seem to have been distorted. According to tradition, local children tie the gates of the church together during marriage services and then demand payment from the newly-weds before they open them again.

At the foot of the church steps, there is an excellent little café called the Cobbled Corner, which serves up delicious home-made food based on produce from farmers in the locality. The café is a popular stopping point for walkers and cyclists, and the well-made wooden tables and chairs are a good advertisement for the one surviving local industry of furniture-making.

The café is well named, because many of the streets in Chipping have cobbled pavements. One such leads to a picturesque corner where there is a seventeenth-century school endowed by John Brabin for the free education of poor children.

On the main street there are two pubs, the Talbot and Tillotsons, which face each other across the road. The Post Office and Craft Centre is housed in a building that is said to have been in use as a shop longer than any other building in the UK.

Do not leave this delightful village without making use of the public toilets on the edge of the car park. The spotless condition of these facilities is a clear indication that the people of Chipping are determined to take care of their charming village. And rightly so!

Bowland Wild Boar Park

The road from Chipping to Dunsop Bridge passes two rather special attractions. Three miles along the road, there is **Bowland Wild Boar Park**. As well as wild boar, the park contains deer, llamas, lambs and goats, all of which can be fed by visiting children. Tractor-pulled barrel rides are another favourite with young visitors, who are also provided with a play area. After all this touchy-feely contact with the animals, it is perhaps disappointing to learn that the café serves home-reared wild boar meat!

The Inn at Whitewell

The second surprise on this road is the **Inn at Whitewell**, a large country inn that began life as a manor house in the Royal Forest of Bowland and was converted to an inn in the eighteenth century. Restored by Richard Bowman, a former Lancashire cricketer and brewer, it is now managed by Charles Bowman. The interior is full of paintings and antiques and the inn's locally-sourced food is famed throughout the land.

This rural gem, which sits above the River Hodder, has 23 guest bedrooms. The proprietors will organise fishing, walking and tutored wine-tastings. In the words of *The Times*, the Inn at Whitewell is 'a well-kept secret in a gorgeous setting amid the misty moors and rolling fells of the Forest of Bowland'.

The Trough of Bowland

Just before the road from Chipping reaches Dunsop Bridge, there is a left turn that leads up and over the moors to the **Trough of Bowland**. Although the route twists and turns, runs along a precipitously narrow ledge and takes a steep descent, it is an absolute must for anyone visiting this area, because it passes through a wild and beautiful landscape with more than a touch of the Scottish Highlands. It is certainly worth driving as far as the whitewashed **Sykes Farm** at the foot of the Trough before retracing your route to the Dunsop Bridge road.

Dunsop Bridge

The village of **Dunsop Bridge** has a very particular claim to fame. A plaque, which was unveiled by Sir Ranulph Fiennes, records that the village is located at the exact centre of Great Britain – a claim verified by the Ordnance Survey.

The Catholic church also has its own claim to fame: it was paid for by Colonel Towneley's prize-money when his horse Kettledrum won the 1861 Derby. With a double-arched bridge, a confluence of fast-flowing streams (the rivers Hodder and Dunsop), a colony of resident ducks and a post office-cum-café-cum-shop called Puddleducks, Dunsop Bridge is a very pretty place indeed. The grassy bank by the stream is a perfect location for a picnic.

Newton-in-Bowland

The road from Dunsop Bridge to Slaidburn passes through **Newton-in-Bowland**, yet another pretty village. This one has a Friends' Meeting House dating from 1767 and a pub called the Parker's Arms, where roaring fires greet travellers seeking warmth, comfort and refreshment. The very best time to visit Newton is Easter, when brightly decorated eggs are to be found in all sorts of unexpected locations in the village.

Slaidburn

The B6478 leads from Newton to the village of **Slaidburn**, which occupies a moorland fold formed by the confluence of Croasdale Brook and the Hodder.

As Slaidburn was once an administrative centre for the Royal Forest of Bowland, minor forest disputes were settled in a courtroom on the upper floor of the Hark to Bounty, which was reached by a staircase that is still attached to the building. The inn acquired its name in 1875, when the local squire heard the howling outside the pub of his favorite hound, Bounty. He turned to his companions and said, 'Hark to Bounty'.

Grey sandstone houses, some of which have carved door-heads, stand behind the kind of cobbled pavements that are such a distinctive feature of Bowland's villages. There is a Heritage Centre, complete with tea room, and a two-storey primary school that was endowed in the will of John Brennand in 1717 and is still in use.

The narrow main street drops down to the banks of the River Hodder, which it crosses by an old stone bridge before heading off to the moors. There is a magnificent view of the surrounding countryside from the square tower of St Andrew's Parish Church, which is of ancient foundation.

Bolton-by-Bowland

Signposts in Slaidburn point to **Bolton-by-Bowland**, yet another stunning village. This one has two village greens, an antique shop, a post office, a tea room and a pub, as well as a bar and restaurant.

The church of St Peter and St Paul has a tower that seems to be far too magnificent for a country village and a remarkable tomb with carvings of Sir Ralph Pudsay, his three wives and 25 children!

Sawley

Before dropping down to the A59, it is worth pausing at Sawley to inspect the ruins of **Sawley Abbey**, which was founded by Cistercian monks in 1147. When the abbey was dissolved in 1537, the monks joined in a revolt known as the Pilgrimage of Grace. As a result, two monks and two local men were hanged at Lancaster, the abbey was sacked of its treasures and the building was all but destroyed. All that remains today is some foundations, a few free-standing walls and a rebuilt entrance arch. Not much to look at, but highly evocative of a turbulent past.

The village is close to the junction with the A59, which provides a fast and direct route back to Preston along the Ribble Valley.

Places to Visit Forest of Bowland

Bowland Wild Boar Park

Chipping
☎ 01995 61554
Open: Easter to Oct 10.30am–5.30pm;
Winter: 11am–4pm

Sawley Abbey

Sawley
☎ 0870 333 1181
Open: 21 Mar to 30 Sept: 10am–6pm;
1 Oct to 21 Mar: 10am–4pm

Slaidburn Heritage Centre

Church Street, Slaidburn
☎ 01200 446161

PLACES TO STAY

Two romantic places to stay:

The Inn at Whitewell

(23 bedrooms; stunning setting)
Near Dunsop Bridge
☎ 01200 448222

Thornley Hall

(self catering; equally stunning setting)
Near Chipping
☎ 01995 61243

PLACES TO EAT

Two very special eating places:

Longridge Restaurant

Longridge
☎ 01772 784969

The Inn at Whitewell

Nr Dunsop Bridge
☎ 01200 448222

TOURIST INFORMATION CENTRES

Bowland Visitor Centre

Beacon Fell Country Park.
☎ 01995 640557

7. Clitheroe & the Ribble Valley

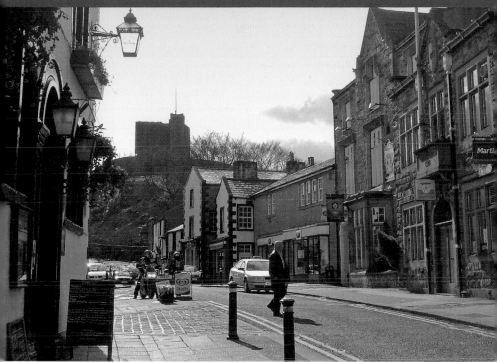

Above: Clitheroe Castle from Castle Street

Clitheroe

The historic market town of **Clitheroe** is not only an excellent touring centre for the Ribble Valley, but also an attractive place in itself.

Although **Clitheroe Castle** is one of the smallest Norman keeps in the country, it manages to dominate the skyline because it stands on the summit of an outcrop of limestone. As a result, the town of Clitheroe has a very striking profile when viewed from the valley. A closer inspection reveals that it is also a town with good specialist shops and fine eating places.

The best starting point for an exploration is the old station building at the foot of King Street. This is now occupied by the **Platform Gallery**, which, as the name suggests, is a platform for contemporary crafts by Lancashire artists. Its bright and attractive gallery space is the venue for eight annual exhibitions, including group, solo and themed shows, with the emphasis on ceramics, textiles and jewellery.

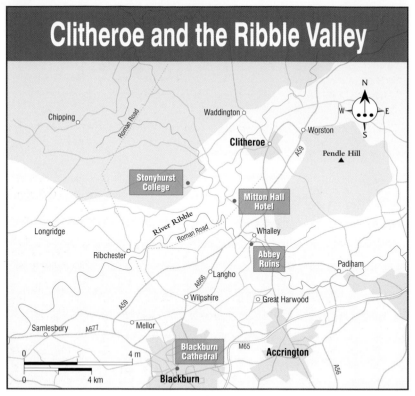

Clitheroe and the Ribble Valley

Across the road from the gallery, there is a noted Clitheroe institution in the shape of **Dawson's**, a family-owned store that sells pottery, garden furniture, bed-linen, towels, giftware, collectables, cookware and barbecues. After browsing in this superb emporium, visitors can relax with a refreshing drink in the store's excellent café and wine bar, which is known as Maxwells.

King Street has a good range of specialist shops, including an attractive florist's called the Floral Basket. An imposing building on the left side of the street is the former post office. It is now occupied by the Old Post House Hotel and a restaurant called the Penny Black, which is also open for tea, coffee and lunches. As well as putting their own stamp on the old postal building, so to speak, the proprietors even run a cycle hire service.

At the summit of King Street, Castle Street runs off to the right and York Street to the left. York Street is the home of a wonderfully-named specialist cheese shop called Cheese Tchaikovsky and also the Olive Press, one of Paul Heathcote's very stylish pizzerias – highly recommended! Castle Street has a good range of shops, including a branch of Boots; Coco Moyo, which sells hand-made chocolates; and Cowman's Famous Sausage Shop, which has 70 varieties of sausage. The street also offers absolutely superb views of the castle, which looms over the buildings in the most picturesque fashion.

Robert de Lacy built the castle in 1186, in order to protect his estates. It is the only remaining fortress in Lancashire that was a Royalist stronghold in the Civil War. The adjacent **Castle Museum** is due to re-open in spring

2009 after an extensive refurbishment.

Rather than diverting along Castle Street or York Street, visitors with a special interest in antiques may wish to continue straight ahead at the summit of King Street. After following a couple of twists and turns, they will arrive at Shawbridge Street, where Miles Griffiths specialises in English antique furniture and decorative antiques, which are on display in a large showroom.

Clitheroe's town-centre shops are supplemented by Booth's and Sainsbury supermarkets.

The Ribble Valley

The River Ribble flows westwards from the Pennines to the Irish Sea, ending its journey in an estuary near Preston. Attractions along the way include several interesting villages; Roman remains; an ancient abbey; a half timbered country house, a college with surprising literary connections; and a celebrated country restaurant.

The valley is bounded by high land, with the extensive moors of the Forest of Bowland stretching along much of its northern flank and the great bulk of Pendle Hill dominating all views to the south.

Waddington

Waddington is located just two miles north-west of Clitheroe. The village often features in calendars because the stream that runs alongside its main street is a gift for photographers looking for a good subject. The stream is crossed by a series of little bridges and flanked

by gardens, where public seats are provided for visitors to relax and enjoy the unusual villagescape views.

Although the village is quite small, it contains three popular pubs: the Waddington Arms, the High Buck and the Lower Buck. The Country Kitchen, which overlooks the stream, is a nice location for refreshments. A scarecrow festival is held during the May Day weekend.

It is said that Henry VI stayed at Waddington Hall for a year before his betrayal by the Yorkists in 1465. He escaped via a secret stairway, only to be captured at Clitheroe.

Stonyhurst College

A country lane runs from Waddington to the Stonyhurst Estate, which is the location for **Stonyhurst College**, a Roman Catholic boarding and day school in the Jesuit tradition.

The school was originally founded in the French city of St Omer in 1593 for English boys who could not obtain a Catholic education in their own country. Persecution of Jesuits in France forced a move to Bruges and then Liège, before the school was established at Stonyhurst in 1794.

The school buildings, which are so vast that they are almost intimidating, include a chapel that is very obviously modelled on King's College Chapel, Cambridge. The college is open to the public during school holidays.

Above: Main Street, Waddington

Middle Earth?

Professor J.R.R. Tolkien was a frequent visitor to Stonyhurst College between 1942 and 1947, because his eldest son John was studying for the priesthood at St Mary's Hall, which is now the prep school for Stonyhurst College.

Tolkien is said to have written part of *Lord of the Rings* in a classroom in the upper gallery of the college and he could well have taken some of his inspiration from the surrounding countryside. Tolkien's son Michael taught Classics at the school in the sixties and seventies.

A further boost to Stonyhurst's literary credentials is that Sir Arthur Conan Doyle was educated at the college!

Great Mitton

The country lane that runs from Stonyhurst College to Whalley crosses the River Hodder via Hodder Lower Bridge, a structure that was built in 1819 and is just a few yards upstream from **Cromwell's Bridge**, a truly re-markable and very picturesque bridge with a very thin, semicircular central arch that has no parapets (do stop to take photographs, but be careful where you park on the bendy road). The story goes that Cromwell's 8,000-strong army crossed over it on 16 August 1648 on their way to the Battle of Preston, which took place on the following day.

Great Mitton clusters around a hilltop that is crowned by an ancient church and an old hall. The Three Fishes and the Aspinall Arms are two fine pubs and eating places within the village and the **Mitton Hall Country House Hotel**, just outside the village, is a large manor house with fabulous food and accommodation in the most atmospheric of surroundings – an old English manor deep in the heart of beautiful countryside!

Whalley

At **Whalley**, there are the remains of a Cistercian abbey, which passed into a ruinous state with the dissolution of the monasteries. In the last century, a country house was built in the grounds. This is now a retreat and conference centre for the Diocese of Blackburn.

However, the abbey gateway has survived, together with extensive foundations and part of the walls of the kitchen, the refectory and the monks' day-room, parlour and vestry. To make up for the lack of buildings, tours are conducted by guides dressed in authentic Cistercian habits. The visitor centre has a coffee shop, an exhibition centre and a gift shop with a nice line in candles and scented soaps.

Langho

By returning to the main road and following it in a westerly direction to its junction with the A666, the visitor is brought to **Langho**, the location for **Northcote Manor**, one of the best country hotels and restaurants in England.

Formerly the residence of a Lancashire cotton baron, the manor was acquired by Nigel Haworth and Craig Bancroft in 1983. The building has

Above left:
Ancient
foundations,
Whalley Abbey

Right: Blackburn
Cathedral

Left: Samlesbury
Hall

14 guest bedrooms and its Michelin-starred restaurant is famed for its fine wines and great food that is based on local produce and traditional Lancashire dishes (especially Lancashire Hotpot) – truly *Cuisine de Terroir*!

A Hotspot For Hotpot

Although Nigel Haworth of Northcote Manor has added a modern twist to Lancashire Hotpot by serving it with oyster beignets, pickled cabbage with star anise and fresh red chillies, he insists that the traditional dish is essentially 'simplicity itself with true, honest flavours'.

Like all the best regional dishes, Lancashire Hotpot was born out of necessity. Hardworking Lancastrians who were strapped for cash needed a meal that would not only supply them with sufficient energy to sustain them through a long day's labour in a cold, damp climate, but would also be cheap to produce and use readily available local ingredients. With a recipe of lamb, chicken stock, onions, potatoes and flour, hotpot filled the bill.

Blackburn

A five-mile (8km) diversion along the A666 to the former mill town of **Blackburn** is surprisingly worthwhile.

Blackburn Cathedral, which took 70 years to complete (1938 to 2008), has a superb central lantern topped by a needle-like aluminium spire. Light filters through scores of panes of coloured glass in the lantern and cascades down to the floor of the crossing like confetti.

On the outside wall of the east end of the church, there is a huge sculpture called **The Healing of the Nations**. By day, it looks like an outsize cushion that has been stuck onto the church in the most incongruous fashion imaginable. However, thousands of interwoven fibre-optics come into play at night, when they produce a dazzling display. On the pavement below, a much smaller sculpture, known as **Grandmother and Child**, depicts a child tugging his grandmother's hand so that he can bend down and retrieve a teddy bear that has fallen on the pavement. Children love this piece of public art and often drag their adult companions to the statue so that they can touch the bronze teddy bear.

While you're in Blackburn, call in **Beee's** on Church Street for the most delicious vanilla scone you'll ever taste and visit **Walsh's Sarsaparilla Bar** in the market, not only for a glass of this Lancashire favourite (see the section on Oldham in the Greater Manchester chapter for more details), but also for many traditional drinks, sweets and remedies. The **Blackburn Museum and Art Gallery** has an eclectic collection, including medieval manuscripts, Japanese prints, Victorian paintings and an Egyptology collection. There are also many artefacts from Blackburn's heyday as a mill town.

Ribchester

A return to the A59, a short journey to the west, followed by a turning to the north leads to **Ribchester**, once the site of a Roman cavalry fort named Bremetannacum Veteranorum.

Many Roman remains have been found, including pottery, inscribed stones, brooches, lamps and even a highly elaborate cavalry helmet. Although the helmet is on display in the British Museum, most of the other finds are exhibited in the **Ribchester Museum**, which stands next to the excavations of a granary established in AD 80 by Agricola.

It is surprising to find that two Roman pillars have been put to good use: one supports the organ loft in the church; the other helps to hold up the porch of the **White Bull**. A second inn in the heart of the village is known as the Black Bull and there are two further inns: the Ribchester Arms and the de Tabley Inn, which stands close to a ford used by Agricola's armies during their advance through the North of England.

As well as possessing a Roman pillar, St Wilfred's Church contains a faded mural to St Christopher, patron saint of travellers, who was often invoked by those about to cross the swift-flowing River Ribble. Unfortunately, he did little to protect the church's first rector, who drowned while undertaking just such a crossing!

Samlesbury

The last port of call on our fascinating journey along the Ribble Valley is **Samlesbury**, some seven miles (11km) west of Ribchester on the A59.

Samlesbury Hall is a highly decorative black-and-white timbered manor house that was built in 1325 by Gilbert de Southworth for his bride-to-be. After some years of neglect, it was restored in the nineteenth century by the Harrison family, who invited their friend Charles Dickens to stay at the hall. After a further restoration by Frederick Baines, the hall fell into disrepair again, but was rescued by a trust in the 1920s. It is open to the public every day except Saturdays, when it is closed for weddings; there is a fine restaurant and 'Henry VIII' gives guided tours every Sunday. Tour guides like dressing up in this part of the world!

The return to Clitheroe is by an easy 13-mile (21km) journey along the A59.

Places to Visit Clitheroe

CLITHEROE

Clitheroe Castle and Museum
Being refurbished at the time of writing – for information Tel: 01200 425111
Likely opening times: weekdays and Sat 11.15am–4pm

Cycle Hire at Old Post House Hotel
King Street ☎ 01200 422025

Platform Gallery
Station Road, Clitheroe
☎ 01200 414556
Open: 10am–4.30pm Mon to Sat

PLACES TO STAY

CLITHEROE

Old Post House Hotel
King Street
☎ 01200 422025

Places to Visit the Ribble Valley

RIBBLE VALLEY

Blackburn Cathedral Shop
Blackburn
☎ 01254 503090
Open: 10.30am–3pm Tue to Sat

Blackburn Museum & Art Gallery
Museum Street
☎ 01254 667130
Open: 9.45am–4.45pm Tue to Fri

Ribchester Museum
Ribchester
☎ 01254 878261
Open: 10am–5pm Mon to Fri; 12pm–5pm at weekends

Samlesbury Hall
Samlesbury
☎ 01254 812010
Open: 11am–4.30pm daily, except Sat when closed for weddings. 'Henry VIII' gives guided tours at 11.15am on Sundays.

Stonyhurst College
Near Great Mitton
☎ 01254 826518
Open: 1pm–4.30pm from third Monday in July to third Monday in August; closed Fri.

Whalley Abbey
Whalley
☎ 01254 828404
Open: 10am–4.30pm daily

PLACES TO STAY

RIBBLE VALLEY

Eaves Hall Country House Hotel
West Bradford
☎ 0844 5027587

Copy Nook Hotel
Bolton by Bowland
☎ 01200 447205

Mitton Hall Country House Hotel
Mitton
☎ 01254 826544

Northcote Manor
Langho
☎ 01254 240555

GREAT PLACES TO EAT

Beee's
Church Street, Blackburn
For great vanilla scones!
☎ 01254 663335

Mitton Hall Country House Hotel
☎ 01254 826544

Northcote Manor
Langho
☎ 01254 240555

TOURIST INFORMATION CENTRES

Blackburn
Church Street
☎ 01254 683536

Clitheroe, Church Walk
☎ 01200 425566

8. Exploring Pendle Hill from Clitheroe

Above: Witches Galore, Newchurch in Pendle

Separated from the Pennine Chain in the east and divided from the Forest of Bowland in the north by the Ribble Valley, Pendle Hill is an isolated, magnificent, brooding presence that dominates the countryside for miles around.

It is not only the spectacular geometry of this great gritstone ridge that grips the imagination, but also its associations with two significant events in the seventeenth century: the notorious trial of the Lancashire witches and the inspirational visitation experienced by George Fox on the summit.

It is customary for hundreds of revellers to capture the spirit of Halloween by walking to the summit at midnight on 31 October, and the bewitching hill is a popular haunt for walkers, photographers and birdwatchers throughout the year.

An anticlockwise circumnavigation of the hill from Clitheroe takes in a magnificent Elizabethan house, a superb heritage centre, a huge modern outlet store, a gift shop dedicated to the Pendle Witches, one of Lancashire's most beautiful villages, a fine garden centre and, of course, stunning views of Pendle Hill at every point of the journey.

Gawthorpe Hall

Gawthorpe Hall stands below the southern slopes of Pendle Hill. It is reached from Clitheroe by heading south-west along the A59 and then turning south-east to Padiham along the A671.

Three storeys high and surmounted by a massive tower, the stone-built hall is a stunning sight and one of England's best-kept secrets. It was built between 1600 and 1605 in a style that bears some resemblance to Hardwick Hall in Derbyshire, which suggests that the architect may have been Robert Smythson.

The hall contains an unrivalled collection of textiles aquired from all over the world by Rachel Kay-Shuttleworth, the last occupant of the hall, and a collection of portraits, many of which are on loan from the National Portrait Gallery. Although its rooms are elaborately furnished and have ornate plasterwork ceilings, the hall manages to combine magnificence with cosiness, a quality that must have appealed to Charlotte Brontë, who was a frequent visitor to the house.

Barrowford

The A6068 runs from **Padiham** to **Barrowford**, a former mill town that also possesses three seventeenth-century mansions. The first of these was used as a refuge by John Wesley when he was attacked by a mob in 1748 and is now a pub called the White Bear. The second has a remarkable triple-decker porch and a cross-wing that features an unusual ogee-shaped window and a carved face designed to ward off witches; it is now the grandest working men's club you are ever likely to see.

The third seventeenth-century mansion is **Park Hill**, which is located close to a fine toll house. It was built in 1561 by the Bannister family and features a picturesque array of gables and mullions. The family fortunes went into sharp decline in the following century, when part of the house was leased to John Swinglehurst, who added an elegant Georgian wing. Sir Roger Bannister, who ran the first four-minute mile, is a direct descendant of the family.

Park Hill is now the home of the **Pendle Heritage Centre**, a superb visitor centre, which includes a reconstructed seventeenth-century parlour with life-size effigies of John and Ellen Bannister, exhibitions that retrace the history of the house and, of course, references to the Pendle Witches.

There is a very comprehensive bookshop and a splendid tea room set in a conservatory that overlooks a carefully restored walled garden. As a bonus, the adjacent barn has been converted into a two-storey art gallery with changing exhibitions of work by professional artists and craftspeople.

As well as being a great place to visit in itself, the centre is the starting point for a number of trails, including the Pendle Way, the Tacklers' Trail, the Water Power Trail and the Witches Trail.

Colne

A short diversion to the outskirts of **Colne** leads to a very different kind of visitor centre. This is the flagship of **Boundary Mill Stores**, which is

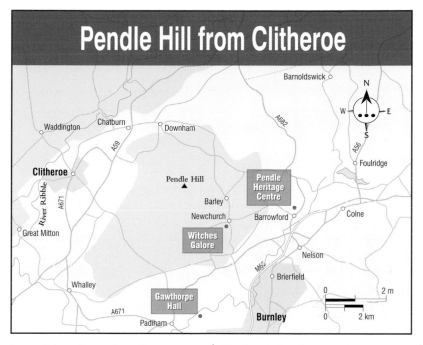

Pendle Hill from Clitheroe

housed in a huge, brand new, two-storey building served by a vast car park. The store is a brand clearance outlet for some 200 top-name brands and includes a cookshop and a large Marks and Spencer outlet.

The coffee shop and restaurant are fronted by a balcony that commands extensive views towards Pendle Hill. In the car park, there is a **Pendle Information Centre** and a 280-seater fish and chip restaurant called Banny's. Little wonder that people come in their droves from all over the country.

The town of Colne is set alongside a pleasant main street that runs along the crest of a long ridge. Its many fine stone buildings include the Town Hall and St Bartholomew's Church, which form a dramatic silhouette when viewed from the valley.

In the churchyard, there is a witch's grave inscribed with nothing more than the initials of the stonemason. The town cemetery contains the grave of Wallace Hartley, the bandmaster who is remembered for asking his musicians to keep playing as the *Titanic* sank.

Newchurch

The village of **Newchurch** is reached most easily by returning to the A6068 and heading back towards Padiham until a signpost for the village appears on the right-hand side of the road.

Newchurch is steeped in memories of evil doings. Close to the church door, there is a grave that is inscribed with a skull and crossbones and is said to be the tomb of Alice Nutter, one of ten 'witches' hanged at Lancaster jail in 1612. The church tower features a strange oval that is known locally as the Eye of God and is supposed to ward off evil spirits.

The village shop, known as **Witches Galore**, sells books, souvenirs, postcards and clothing related to witches – as well as drinks and ice cream!

Above left: Gawthorpe Hall Above right: Witches Galore, Newchurch in Pendle

Below: Downham, Lancashire prettiest village

Above: Old Well Hall, Tudor house in Downham

Right: Pendle Hill from Downham

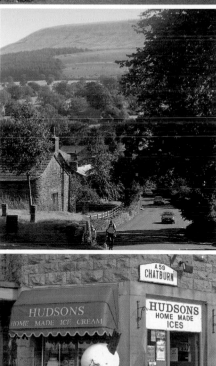

Above: The Assheton Arms, Downham

Right: Hudson's home-made ice cream, Chatburn

The Best of Lancashire

The Pendle Witches

In the early years of the seventeenth century, there lived in the Pendle area two rival families known as the Demdikes and the Chattoxes. Each family had such a bad reputation for begging and extortion that the locals considered their female members to be witches, operating under the evil influence of two matriarchs known as Old Demdike and Old Chattox.

In 1612, Alizon Device, the granddaughter of Old Demdike, cursed a pedlar when he refused to give her some pins. The pedlar collapsed, either from fright or because he had been attacked by the girl's dog. His nephew reported the incident to the police, who promptly questioned Alizon.

Amazingly, she not only gave a full confession, but also implicated other members of her family, as well as members of the rival Chattox family. When more people were questioned, they either confessed, perhaps hoping to receive lenient sentences, or implicated others to save their own skins. As a result, a dozen people were arrested and sent to Lancaster jail to await trial as suspected witches. Old Demdike died in prison, but ten of the others were convicted and hanged.

Barley

After leaving Newchurch, the road passes through the village of **Barley** as it heads towards the eastern lip of Pendle Hill.

Barley is the most popular starting point for walks up Pendle Hill, either by the easy route by the reservoirs or by the more difficult climb straight up to the 'Big End' of the hill. The village provides plenty of opportunities for walkers to fortify themselves before the climb. As well as tea rooms, there is a pub called the Pendle Inn and a restaurant called the Barley Mow. George Fox undertook the climb in 1652 and claims to have experienced a visitation on the summit that inspired him to start the Quaker movement.

The four-mile (6.5km) drive from Barley to **Downham** is one of the most spectacular in England. The Big End of Pendle dominates views to the left, while a vast panorama unfolds ahead and to the right. After climbing to a summit, the road drops steeply to the village of Downham.

Downham

Nestling in its sleepy hollow below the great bulk of Pendle Hill, Downham is generally considered to be Lancashire's prettiest village. Ever since 1559, the entire settlement has been in the hands of the Asshetons, who have always treated the place with tender loving care. They restored the medieval church, added a Regency façade to the hall and built the school, the vicarage and most of the estate cottages. The present members of the family have preserved the skyline by banning television aerials, satellite dishes and even dormer windows.

The church, the hall and the Assheton Arms are grouped around a green at the top end of the village street, which descends a steep incline to Downham

Beck, providing fabulous views of Pendle Hill along the way.

By the beck, there is a second green surrounded by a picturesque cluster of cottages, including Old Well Hall, a Tudor house with mullioned windows and a projecting porch. A stone bridge and the village stocks complete a perfect composition. Downham was used as a location for the classic film *Whistle down the Wind*.

Chatburn

The return journey to the A59 passes through **Chatburn**, where many will be tempted to call in at Hudson's for delicious home-made ice cream, while others will head for the splendid restaurant at Shackleton's Garden Centre.

Clitheroe is reached by making a journey of two miles (3km) along the A59.

Places to Visit Pendle Hill Area

Boundary Mill Stores

Vivary Way, Colne
☎ 01282 856200
Open: 10am–10pm Mon to Fri; 9am 6pm Sat, 10am 5pm Sun

Discover Pendle

On Boundary Mill Stores site
☎ 01282 856186

Gawthorpe Hall (N.T)

Padiham
☎ 01282 771004
Open: 1pm–5pm every day from Apr to Oct, except Mon and Fri

Pendle Heritage Centre

Park Hill, Barrowford
☎ 01282 661702
Open: 10am–5pm daily except Christmas Day

Witches Galore

Newchurch
☎ 01282 61311
Open: 11am–5pm apart from Wed when 1.30pm–5pm

TOURIST INFORMATION CENTRES

BARROWFORD
Pendle Heritage Centre
☎ 01282 661702

COLNE
Discover Pendle
Boundary Mill Stores
☎ 01282 856186

9. Liverpool

Thanks to its two magnificent cathedrals, its iconic waterfront, its great architectural heritage (more listed buildings than any British city outside London and more Georgian buildings than Bath), its plethora of theatres, its world-class museums and galleries, its huge shopping area, its sporting traditions and its world renown as the birthplace of the Beatles, **Liverpool** is a major tourist destination.

The city's Georgian prosperity was largely founded on slavery, with 80 per cent of Britain's slave commerce and 40 per cent of the European slave trade passing through Liverpool in the eighteenth century. In the following century, the city became one of the greatest ports in the world, with 40 per cent of the world's trade passing through its docks.

By 1917, when all the 'Three Graces' (the Liver Building, the Port of Liverpool Building and the Cunard Building) had been constructed on the city's waterfront, the first sight of Liverpool by those arriving from the sea was on a par with the first sight of New York for those crossing the Atlantic in the opposite direction. Indeed, in many ways Liverpool was Britain's New York.

During the last century, the city's fortunes have taken a roller coaster ride. Liverpool was badly bombed in the Second World War, when 2,500 of its citizens were killed; two decades later, with the emergence of the Beatles and the Merseybeat sound, the city became the most important centre of popular music in the world; in the 1970s, with the advent of containerisation, the docks went into a sharp decline and the unemployment rate soared; since the beginning of the 1990s, Liverpool has been steadily regenerated; in 2008,

it re-emerged on the world stage as the European Capital of Culture.

To celebrate the city's year of glory, a giant mechanical spider known as La Princesse roamed the streets, discharging a range of special effects, including rain, flame, smoke, wind, snow, light and sound. Although some arachnophobics kept well away from Liverpool while La Princesse was on the march, it would take more than a mechanical spider to keep away the thousands of Beatles fans, sports fans, architecture buffs, art lovers and theatre-goers who enjoy visiting this fascinating city.

The city has four fairly distinct areas: the cathedral and university quarter; the cultural quarter; the shopping centre and the area around the Albert Dock and the Pier Head. We'll begin our exploration at the cathedrals, which are the first major structures to be seen by travellers approaching the city from the M62 motorway or the East Lancashire Road.

Top Tips Liverpool

• For a study in contrasts, visit the ultra-modern Roman Catholic Cathedral and the much more traditionally styled Anglican Cathedral.

• Pop into Mr Hardman's Home Photographic Studio on Rodney Street and see his shots of the city when it was the gateway to the Empire.

• Sample Russian cuisine at the St Petersburg Restaurant.

• See the great paintings in the Walker Art Gallery and guess how the boy reacted to the question: 'And when did you last see your father?'

• See a production at one of Liverpool's theatres – you might be lucky enough to spot the next in a long line of great actors and playwrights to emerge from the city.

• Do you rate modern art or dismiss it? Decide for yourself at the Tate Modern.

• Liverpool is packed with brilliant museums – firstly visit one with a theme that matches your particular interests and then visit one that will tell you something new.

• Discover all there is to know about the Fab Four at the Beatles Story in the Albert Dock.

• Take an amphibious trip on the Yellow Duckmarine.

• Shop until you drop in Liverpool One, the huge new shopping complex.

The Cathedral Quarter

Liverpool's two cathedrals are well sign-posted from the East Lancashire Road and the M62 motorway. The **Roman Catholic Cathedral of Christ the King** (also known as the Metropolitan Cathedral) comes into full view immediately after the approach road into the city passes the first university buildings. Its appearance is very striking, because it bears more than a superficial resem-

blance to a giant space capsule. Its tall lantern is supported by a ring of flying buttresses, which also subdivide the various chapels on the circumference of the church. The altar is on a raised platform in the centre and the congregation is placed 'in the round'.

The starkness of the concrete is alleviated by the fine stained-glass windows in the chapels and, more especially, by the spectacular coloured light display that emanates from the lantern, where the stained glass was designed by John Piper.

This uncompromisingly modern church, known by many Liverpudlians as 'Paddy's Wigwam', bears absolutely no resemblance to the building that was proposed by Sir Edwin Lutyens in the early years of the twentieth century. His plan included what would have been the biggest dome in the world, as well as barrel-vaulted naves and aisles, with 53 chapels lining the nave and transepts.

Although the crypt was completed to Lutyens' designs, spiralling costs put paid to the realisation of the rest of his proposals. Adrian Gilbert Scott, the brother of the architect of the Anglican Cathedral, which was rising slowly at the other end of Hope Street, was asked to come up with a scaled-down version of the Lutyens project, but even this proved far too costly.

In the end, it was decided to hold an architectural competition for a modern church that could be completed within five years at a reasonable cost. Sir Frederick Gibberd's design was chosen out of the 300 that were submitted and his church was duly completed within the space of five years (1962 to 1969) at a fraction of the cost of the Lutyens cathedral. Today, it stands as a rare example of a successful concrete building from the sixties and as a perfect foil for the Gothic Anglican Cathedral at the other end of Hope Street.

The Anglican **Cathedral Church of Christ** is the largest cathedral in Britain. It was designed in 1903 by 22-year-old Giles Gilbert Scott. Although work began just one year later, the church was not completed until 1978.

Now often marketed as the 'Great Space', the interior combines the height of a Gothic cathedral with the width of a Classical church. In fact, the interior space is truly awesome. The Lady Chapel at the head of the south aisle is virtually a church in itself and even has its own organ.

Notable features within the building include a nave bridge, which looks remarkably like that in London's Natural History Museum, and a huge painting of the Good Samaritan by Adrian Wiszniewski. The cathedral's architect, Giles Gilbert Scott, also designed the iconic red telephone box, an example of which is on display in the church. There is an excellent bookshop, a restaurant that has won Egon Ronay accolades and a new mezzanine coffee shop.

The cathedral's peal of bells is the highest and heaviest in the world and the balcony above the west door supports a very powerful sculpture of the **Welcoming Christ** by Dame Elisabeth Frink.

Before proceeding to the Cultural Quarter, it is worth walking along Rodney Street to **Mr Hardman's Home Photographic Studio,** where E. Chambré Hardman lived and worked. Displays of his photographic work reflect the days when Liverpool was the gateway to the British Empire and the world.

Cultural Quarter

Liverpool's **Cultural Quarter** is centred around William Brown Street on the northern edge of the city centre. The most magnificent buildings in the area are **St George's Hall** and the **Walker Art Gallery.**

St George's Hall dominates the Cultural Quarter from its elevated island site rather like the Parthenon dominates Athens. In fact, it is closely modelled on a Greek temple and has been called the finest neoclassical building in the world. Since the completion of a £23 million restoration project in 2007, the building has welcomed visitors into its museum, its tea room and its viewing gallery, which has magnificent views into the auditorium of the Great Hall.

The **Walker Art Gallery** has a great collection of fine and decorative art spanning six centuries. Its many great paintings include: *And when did you last see your father?* by William Frederick Yeames; *Isabella* by John Everett Millais; *Self Portrait as a Young Boy* by Rembrandt; *Peter Getting out of Nick's Pool* by David Hockney and *Interior at Paddington* by Lucian Freud. Could art lovers wish for more?!

The adjacent **Central Library** symbolises the cultural legacy of the city's merchants. It includes the double-decker Hornby Library with a collection bequeathed by Hugh Frederick Hornby; the Picton Reading Room, which is based on the rotunda of the British Museum; and the Oak Room, which contains 4,000 rare books.

The final building in this superb Cultural Quarter is the **World Museum**, which uses the latest interactive technology and is one of the finest multi-disciplinary museums in the UK, with exhibits covering the natural and human world and the earth in space and time.

The Shopping District

Liverpool's extensive shopping area has recently been expanded yet further by the opening of **Liverpool One**, a £920 million development containing 160 new shops, cafés and restaurants, as well as two new hotels, a 14-screen cinema and 600 stylish apartments.

Elsewhere in the shopping district, there is a great choice of high-street styles on Church Street, Clayton Square and in St John's Shopping Centre. Fashion hotspots include Cavern Walks, Bold Street and the Met Quarter.

Williamson Square, at the heart of the shopping district, is overlooked by a giant communications tower and by the **Playhouse Theatre**, which, together with the **Everyman** (near the Cultural Quarter), has nurtured a remarkably strong cast of talented actors and playwrights from the city, including Julie Walters, Rex Harrison, Rita Tushingham, Willy Russell and Alan Bleasdale. As well as the Playhouse and Everyman, Liverpool's theatre venues include the Empire, the Royal Court, the Unity Theatre, the Liverpool Olympia and the Philharmonic Hall.

Two unexpected finds in the shopping district are **Bluecoat**, a beautiful eighteenth-century school building, which has now been converted into an arts centre, and **The National Conservation Centre**, where it is possible to find out how everything is conserved, from Egyptian mummies to classic motorbikes.

Albert Dock and Pier Head

Our final destination in Liverpool takes us to the bank of the Mersey and the **Albert Dock**, a UNESCO World Heritage site, where the world's first enclosed, non-combustible dock

Top left: Anglican Cathedral   Right: Liver Building and globe

Middle: Merseyside Maritime Museum, Albert Dock

Bottom left: The Beatles Story, Albert Dock   Right: Yellow Duckmarine, Albert Dock

warehouse system, constructed in cast iron, brick and stone, has been restored and transformed into apartments and a major tourist destination, with a range of shops, eating places, offices, luxury apartments and hotels. There is also a very impressive list of museums, exhibitions and galleries within the dock.

Tate Liverpool is the home of the National Collection of Modern Art. As well as staging displays from the Tate collection, it mounts major exhibitions of modern and contemporary art. In fact, it is one of the largest and most important galleries of modern art in the UK, outside London.

Liverpool Maritime Museum mounts displays that tell of Liverpool's role as a major port and gateway to the New World. One gallery tells the tragic stories of the *Titanic*, the *Lusitania* and the *Empress of Ireland*; another room is devoted to the Merchant Navy and the lifelines it has provided in times of war and peace; there is a display covering the Battle of the Atlantic and the basement is devoted to smuggling!

The **International Slavery Museum** is aimed at promoting a better understanding of the source of much of Liverpool's wealth: transatlantic slavery, which involved the greatest forced migration in history. The museum is a graphic testimony to the resilience and spirit of the people who endured enslavement. Some of the stories of their bravery and rebellion are very remarkable.

The former **Piermaster's House** has been transformed into one of Liverpool's smallest but most fascinating visitor attractions, because it has been refurnished as a house from World War II. With its head-to-toe beds, chamber pots, ration books in the kitchen and basic furniture, this is highly evocative of the days before labour-saving devices and decent wages became available to the masses.

Last, but not least, we come to **The Beatles Story**, which aims to transport visitors back to the life, times, culture and music of the Beatles' era. In the Discovery Zone, children can select a song at a record store from the fifties, when the Quarrymen were evolving into the Beatles, or play a Beatles tune on a piano or create Beatles artwork. As one would expect, there is a well-stocked Fab Four Store.

Continuing with the Beatles theme, visitors can take a ride, on both land and water, in an amphibious World War II landing craft, now relaunched and rebranded as the **Yellow Duck-marine**!

The Beatles may have been the most famous of the Liverpool pop stars, but another Liverpool singing legend, Billy Fury, is commemorated by a sculpture on the riverside promenade that leads to the **Three Graces** (the Liver Building, with its two Liver Birds, the Cunard Building and the Port of Liverpool Building). It's impossible not to stare up in wonder and admiration at these imposing early twentieth-century buildings, so diverse in character, but so harmonious as a group.

And what better way to end your trip to this great city than by taking a 'Ferry across the Mersey'? The views from the boat back towards the city and its famous skyline are unforgettable.

Places to Visit Liverpool

Anglican Cathedral
Upper Duke Street
☎ 0151 709 6271
Open daily: 8am–6pm

Bluecoat Art Centre
School Lane
☎ 0151 702 5324
Open: 10am–5.30pm Mon to Sat; 12pm–5pm Sun; 9am–5pm Bank Holidays

International Slavery Museum
Albert Dock
☎ 0151 478 4499
Open: daily 10am–5pm

Liverpool Maritime Museum
Albert Dock
☎ 0151 478 4499
Open: daily 10am–5pm

Metropolitan Cathedral (RC)
Hope Street
☎ 0151 709 9222
Open: 8am–6pm. Closes at 5pm on Sun in winter

Mr Hardman's Home Photographic Studio
Rodney Street
☎ 0151 709 6261
Open: Mar to Nov 11am–4.15pm Wed to Sun; Nov to Dec 11am–4.15pm Sat, Sun

National Conservation Centre
Whitechapel
☎ 0151 478 4999
Open: daily 10am–5pm

Piermaster's House
Albert Dock
☎ 0151 478 4499
Open: daily 10am–3.30pm

St George's Hall
William Brown Street
☎ 0151 225 6909
Open: 10am–5pm Tue to Sat; 1pm–5pm Sun

The Beatles Story
Albert Dock
☎ 0151 709 1963
Open: daily 9am–7pm

Tate Liverpool
Albert Dock
☎ 0151 702 7400
Open: Oct to Mar: 10am–5.30pm, closed Mon except Bank Holiday.
Apr to Sep: 10am–5.30pm Mon to Sun

Walker Art Gallery
William Brown Street
☎ 0151 478 4199
Open: daily 10am–5pm

Places to Visit Liverpool

World Museum
William Brown Street
☎ 0151 478 4393
Open: daily 10am–5pm

Yellow Duckmarine
Albert Dock
☎ 0151 708 7799
Tours commence daily at 10.30am

THEATRES, CONCERT HALLS

To discover what's on in all the Liverpool theatres and concert halls, visit www.liverpooltheatreguide.com

HOTELS

There is a very wide range of hotels in Liverpool, including a themed hotel called The Liner and the inevitable Hard Day's Night Hotel. The best bet for visitors planning an overnight stay is to consult the internet.

YOUTH HOTEL

Liverpool
25, Tabley St (off Wapping) L1 8EE
☎ 0870 770 5924

RESTAURANTS

Liverpool is blessed with a huge number of good restaurants. Some of the best include: The Olive Press on Castle Street; Simply Heathcotes at Beetham Plaza; The Monro Gastro Pub on Duke street; Chung Ku on Columbus Quay; Hamiltons (founded by Atomic Kitten Natasha Hamilton) in the Met Quarter; The Living Room in Victoria Street; Nando's (for Portuguese cuisine) in Liverpool One; Sapporo Teppanyaki (for Japanese cuisine) on Duke Street; and St Petersburg Russian Restaurant on York Street.

SHOPPING

The prime shopping areas are: Liverpool One; Church Street; Clayton Square; St John's Shopping Centre; and for fashions Cavern Walks, Bold Street and the Met quarter.

TOURIST INFORMATION CENTRES

The O8 Place
Whitechapel
☎ 0151 233 2008

Maritime Museum
Albert Dock
☎ 0151 233 2008

John Lennon Airport
☎ 0151 233 2008

Above: Making friends with one of Antony Gormley's 'iron men', Crosby

Our final chapter picks out ten highlights of Merseyside and West Lancashire.

Although the metropolitan county of Merseyside covers land on both sides of the Mersey estuary, we'll confine ourselves to the northern coastal regions that are still associated in most people's minds with Lancashire. This stretch of coast takes in a beach populated with one hundred iron men, a coastal path with famous geological features and one of England's most elegant coastal resorts.

After journeying along the coast, we take a clockwise loop through West Lancashire, a region of green countryside and market gardens, a considerable part of which has had to be drained from the marshes. For example, the village of Tarleton, which stands on a low hill, was once an island.

In the course of our journey, we visit a town whose church has a spire detached from its tower, a small village that is a surprising centre of culinary excellence, two half-timbered country houses, a theme park with wizards and battling knights, a famous wildfowl park and a safari park with a huge collection of animals ranging from American bison to Asian camels.

Crosby

The village of **Crosby** is located seven miles (11km) north of Liverpool and stands by a right-angled bend on the A565. It is a favoured place of residence and has a busy shopping centre that includes Steve Pritchard's superb independent bookshop and Satterthwaite's famous craft bakery, which specialises in Liverpool Cakes produced from a recipe for Liverpool Tart that was discovered in the West Country, of all places!

The town is also famous as the home of Edward Smith, captain of the *Titanic*, and Arthur Rostron, captain of the *Carpathia*, which took on board 712 survivors when the *Titanic* was sunk by an iceberg.

However, the main reason for visiting Crosby is its four-mile (6km) long stretch of sandy beach, which is populated by 100 life-size iron men produced by the sculptor Antony Gormley. Collectively, the men, who stare impassively out to sea, form an installation called ***Another Place***.

Originally intended as a temporary exhibit, the sculptures now have a permanent place on the beach. As the tides ebb and flow, the figures become submerged and exposed by turn. Whatever the state of the tide, they have a mesmeric effect on all who see them, causing their observers to become transfixed in a seaward stare like that of the iron men themselves!

A 13-mile (21km) journey along the A656 connects Crosby with Southport. The two towns are also connected by the 12-mile (20km) **Sefton Coastal Path**, *which runs through nature reserves, woods, beaches and sand dunes.*

Southport

Lord Street, Southport's main shopping street, is an elegant, arcaded boulevard that is said to have inspired Louis-Napoléon Bonaparte to create the boulevards of Paris. Although Lord Street runs parallel with the seafront, it is a long way from the street to the promenade. It is even further (at most times of the month) from the promenade to the sea!

However, this is all part of Southport's attraction. The gap between Lord Street and the promenade contains a lake that is a venue for all manner of water-based activities, a Splash World, which has high-speed water slides, lazy river rapids, water cannons and water curtains, a beautiful old carousel and an amusement park with rides that range from gentle to white-knuckle.

The water areas that divide the shopping area from the front are connected by a superbly designed Marine Way Bridge and the land is connected to the sea by a fine pier, which is the second longest in Britain and has a tourist train running along its full length.

When the sea is out, which is most of the time, the huge flat sandy beach is part car park and part children's paradise for sandcastle making, kite flying, football, beach cricket and a host of other activities. On the rare occasions when the sea comes in, everyone seems determined to celebrate its arrival by jumping in *en masse*.

Southport stages a very impressive range of annual events, including a Food and Drink Festival, a Musical Firework Championship, an Air Show and the famous **Southport Flower Show**.

Royal Birkdale Golf Course, a links course that covers the dunes to the south of the resort, has been a venue for both the Open Championship and the Ryder Cup.

The village of Tarleton is nine miles (15km) east of Southport and is reached by following the A565.

Tarleton

Once upon a time, **Tarleton** was an island in the Lancashire marshes. Today, it is a neat residential village with some attractive old cottages set alongside the ever-expanding streets of new houses: a place that is unremarkable in appearance, but worth visiting for three reasons.

Firstly, the village is surrounded by market gardens, which thrive on the rich soil left behind when the marshes were drained. **Dunscar Garden Centre**, which has been managed by the same family for three generations, is a splendid destination, not only because it has a very fine range of plants and garden accessories, but also because its café enjoys ready access to local produce and has deservedly gained a North West Fine Foods Award. When visiting the garden centre, don't forget to ask to see a piece of bog-oak that has led some experts to suggest that the waters that once covered much of the area were the result of a tsunami!

Secondly, almost all the village shops, from the delicatessen, bakery and butchers to the furniture store, are long-established, family-run businesses – perhaps this is a historical legacy from the days when the people had to be self-reliant because Tarleton was an island. **Webster and Sons**, a high-quality furnishing store, which has been dubbed 'the Harrods of the North', was founded in 1889 by Joseph Webster. It is now in the hands of his great-grandson. The store includes a very popular restaurant.

Thirdly, Tarleton was without a church for many years until the construction of **St Mary's Church** in

1717. Built in red brick, with a later stone tower, it is preserved by the Churches' Conservation Trust, but is now only used for services on the fourth Sunday in August, because it was replaced in the late nineteenth century by a new church that was more conveniently located in the centre of the village.

The Camelot Theme Park is 12 miles (19km) from Tarleton. It is reached by taking the A59, followed by the A5209 to Charnock Richard.

Camelot Theme Park

The **Camelot Theme Park** boasts something for everyone, from tots to adults. Twice per day, Merlin performs his illusions in the castle and there is even a 20-minute wizard workshop for adults and children, where visitors can

Top left: Georgian Church, Tarleton

Left: Lord Street, Southport

Bottom left: The pier, Southport

Above: Martin Mere

Above: Ormskirk

*Right: Speke Hall,
near Liverpool*

learn how to perform their own tricks. There are regular displays of medieval jousting and children can meet the animals on Squire Bumpkin's Farm. Fairground rides range from gentle children's rides to a whirlwind-spinning roller coaster and log flumes.

On a rather gentler note, nearby **Park Hall** holds a large antique fair every Sunday.

As a point of interest, the Charnock Richard service station was the very first service station on the M6 when it opened in 1963.

The village of Wrightington, just 3.5

miles (5.5km) south of the Camelot Theme Park, is reached by taking the A49 followed by the B5250.

Wrightington

Although it is located only a stone's throw from the M6 motorway, **Wrightington** is an attractive residential village set in very pleasant countryside. However, the main reason for making a visit to the village is food – and what food!

Village lad Mark Prescott trained as a chef at the Chester Grosvenor, the

Waterside Inn at Bray and Le Gavroche, before returning to his home village and establishing the **Mulberry Tree**. Mark has made this former pub into one of the North West's great eating places and won lots of awards along the way.

This gastronomic village also contains the White Lion, which is a pub and restaurant, a Simply Heathcote's restaurant, the High Moor Restaurant, which has traditional cuisine with a modern twist, and the Rygby Arms country inn and bistro.

For an interesting walk to work off all that food, head for **Tunley Parish Church** at Mossy Lea. Built in 1691, it is the oldest Presbyterian church in England.

A journey of some 9 miles (15km) in a westerly direction along the A5209 leads to Martin Mere.

Martin Mere

Martin Mere, which is run by the Wildfowl and Wetlands Trust, is a hugely popular attraction set around 50 acres (20 hectares) of landscaped waterfowl gardens. The grounds are a home for thousands of over-wintering swans, geese and other wildfowl, including 22 of the world's 40 most endangered species. There is a play area, an excellent visitor centre and gift shop, and a Pinkfoot Pantry that has gained Taste Lancashire Quality Assurance accreditation.

All in all, Martin Mere offers a great day out for the whole family. It is a great favourite with young children, and wildfowl photographers love the place because the opportunities for close-up shots are endless.

Rufford Old Hall is just 3 miles (5km) along the A59.

Rufford Old Hall

Rufford Old Hall is one of Lancashire's best Tudor buildings. Standing in the midst of fine topiary, it has a very elaborate half-timbered wing juxtaposed at right angles to a brick wing.

The most spectacular feature of the interior is the Great Hall, where Shakespeare is thought to have performed. The room has a hammer-beam roof and a decorated wooden screen. Rufford also contains a noted collection of arms and armoury.

Ormskirk lies six miles (10km) south along the A59.

Ormskirk

Ormskirk is a pleasant town with a thriving stall market. However, its chief attraction is the **Parish Church of St Peter and St Paul**, which is built on a sandstone outcrop and has the very unusual distinction of having a tower that is separate from the steeple.

According to legend, Orme had two sisters, one of whom wanted a tower, the other a spire. To please them both, he built both. Nice story, but untrue: the tower dates from 1548, when it was built to house the bells from Burscough Priory, and the spire dates from 1832, when it was built to replace a fifteenth-century steeple that had burnt down.

As a matter of interest, the only other churches in England to have a tower separated from a steeple are both in Wiltshire.

The church contains memorials to two significant members of the Stanley family: Thomas Stanley, who changed sides at the Battle of Bosworth in 1485 and caused Richard III to lose his crown, and James Stanley, a Royalist who was beheaded at Bolton in 1651 after the Civil War – his body is buried in one tomb and his head in a separate casket!

Knowsley is 11 miles (18km) from Orm-skirk. The route is via the A59, the A5036 and the B5194.

Knowsley Safari Park

Knowsley Hall, the seat of the Stanley family, is a magnificent mansion set in 2,500 acres (1,000 hectares) of parkland that was landscaped by Capability Brown. The house is available for hire for weddings, conferences and business meetings, but is only open to the general public for a few days each August.

In 1971, the Earl of Derby opened an animal park that was closely modelled on African reserves, in that it allowed animals to roam freely while their observers sat in cages (their cars). This set a trend that has been followed in many other places in the country.

In its original form, **Knowsley Safari Park** contained lions, cheetahs, monkeys, baboons, giraffes, zebras, elephants and antelopes. After proving enormously popular, the park was extended in 1973 to allow the introduction of camels, buffalo, white rhino and tigers.

Every attempt is made to display the animals in surroundings that are as near natural as possible. Endangered species are regularly introduced as a

matter of policy – for example, recent arrivals include some very rare African wild dogs. The new education centre encourages all visitors to learn about the fragility and importance of the earth's ecosystems. Little wonder that the safari park, which involves a five-mile (8km) drive around the grounds, attracts half a million visitors per year.

Speke Hall is reached from Knowsley by a 13-mile (21km) journey, via the A5300, followed by the A562 and the A561.

Speke Hall

With its superb black-and-white, half-timbered exterior, Speke Hall is an outstanding example of a Tudor half-timbered house, but the interior comes as something of a surprise – a delightful one if you like Victorian furnishings; a disappointing one if you don't.

In fairness, the interior does have elements from other periods, including Jacobean plasterwork, a Tudor Great Hall and a priest hole, dating from the days when the Catholic Norris family lived there.

Since 1943, the house has been administered by the National Trust, which has acquired part of the grounds to prevent further encroachments on the house's setting. Before the Trust stepped in, one area had already been sold off to allow the construction of Speke Airport, which is now known as John Lennon Airport.

This visit to a Tudor mansion that stands next to a modern facility that has been renamed in honour of one of Liverpool's most famous sons is a fitting end to our travels.

Places to Visit in Merseyside and West Lancashire

Camelot Theme Park

Charnock Richard
☎ 01257 452100
Times vary. See www.camelotthemepark.
co.uk

Dunscar Garden Centre

Tarleton
☎ 01772 812684
Open: 9am–6pm Mon to Sat; 1.30
am–4.30pm Sun

Knowsley Safari Park

Prescot
☎ 0151 430 9009
Open: Mar to Oct 10am–4pm; Nov to
Feb 10.30am–3pm

Martin Mere Wildfowl and Wetlands Trust

Martin Mere
☎ 01704 895181
Open: winter 9.30am–5pm, summer
9.30am–5.30pm

Mulberry Tree Restaurant

Wrightington
☎ 01257 451400

Rufford Old Hall

Liverpool Road
☎ 01704 821254
Open: Mar to Oct 1pm–5pm each day
except Thu, Fri

Southport Flower Show

Victoria Park
☎ 01704 547147
Takes place in August

Speke Hall

Speke
☎ 01257 451400
Open: Mar to Oct 1pm–5.30pm Wed to
Sun; Nov to midpDec 1pm–4.30pm on
Sat, Sun only.

TOURIST INFORMATION CENTRE

Southport

Lord Street
☎ 01704 533333

Index

Index